NOV   2009

W9-CQW-119

Loving v. Virginia:

LIFTING THE BAN AGAINST INTERRACIAL MARRIAGE

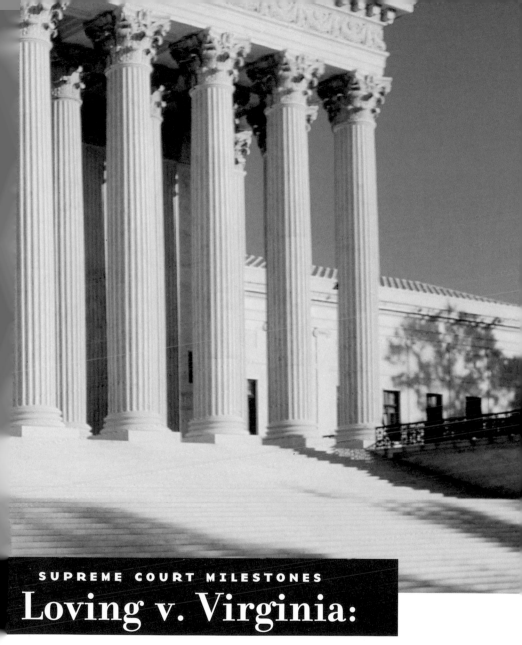

SUPREME COURT MILESTONES

Loving v. Virginia:

LIFTING THE BAN AGAINST INTERRACIAL MARRIAGE

SUSAN DUDLEY GOLD

Marshall Cavendish
Benchmark
New York

*For Tamara Moxham, with appreciation for her good humor
and her enthusiasm in embracing the differences in us all*

Marshall Cavendish Benchmark
99 White Plains Road
Tarrytown, NY 10591
www.marshallcavendish.us

Library of Congress Cataloging-in-Publication Data

Gold, Susan Dudley.
 Loving v. Virginia : lifting the ban against interracial marriage / by Susan Dudley Gold.
    p. cm. — (Supreme Court milestones)
 Includes bibliographical references and index.
 ISBN 978-0-7614-2586-1
 1. Loving, Richard Perry—Trials, litigation, etc.—Juvenile literature.
 2. Loving, Mildred Jeter—Trials, litigation, etc.—Juvenile literature.
 3. Interracial marriage—Law and legislation—Virginia—Juvenile literature.
 [1. Loving, Richard Perry—Trials, litigation, etc. 2. Loving, Mildred
 Jeter—Trials, litigation, etc. 3. Interracial marriage.] I. Title. II. Series.

  KF224.L68G65 2007
  346.7301'6—dc22

2006035955

Photo research by Connie Gardner

Cover Photo: Bill Heinsohn/Alamy

The photographs in this book are used by permission and through the courtesy of:
Alamy: Bill Heinsohn, 2-3; *AP Photo*: 6; Bill Hudson, 12; *Getty Images*:
Stringer/Time/Life Pictures, 11; Carl Iwasaki/Time Life Pictures, 32; Grey Villet/Time
Life Pictures, 39,42,47,58; Judith Gefter/Pix Inc/Time Life Pictures, 45; MPI, 70;
Hulton Archive, 82; Judith Whitmore/Time Life Pictures, 89; Nat Farbman/Time Life
Pictures, 104; *Corbis*: L. Seaman, 14; Arnold Genthe, 79; Bettmann, 92,108; Hulton
Deutsch Collection, 99; *The Granger Collection*: 16.

Publisher: Michelle Bisson
Art Director: Anahid Hamparian
Series Designer: Sonia Chaghatzbanian
Printed in China
1 3 5 6 4 2

contents

one   When Marriage Is a Criminal Act   7

TWO   Laws Against Interracial Marriage   15

THree   Campaign for Civil Rights   31

four   Back in Court   43

FIVe   Making Their Case   57

SIX   Before the Court   73

seven   Decision and Aftermath   105

Notes   121

Further Information   131

Bibliography   135

Index   140

MILDRED AND RICHARD LOVING ARE ALL SMILES AT A PRESS CONFERENCE ON JUNE 13, 1967, THE DAY AFTER THE SUPREME COURT RULED IN THEIR FAVOR IN *LOVING V. VIRGINIA*.

one
WHEN MARRIAGE IS A
CRIMINAL ACT

AT 2 a.m. on June 12, 1958, as Richard Perry Loving and Mildred Jeter Loving lay sleeping in their bed in her parents' home in Central Point, Virginia, the sheriff and two deputies barged into their room and shone flashlights into their terrified faces. Caroline County Sheriff R. Garnett Brooks demanded of Richard, "What are you doing in bed with this lady?"

The young man mutely pointed to the marriage certificate hanging on the bedroom wall.

"That's no good here," the sheriff responded. With that, he arrested the young couple, charging them with miscegenation, or intermarriage between people of different races.

Ten days before, on June 2, the pair had traveled to Washington, D.C., about one hundred miles from the Virginia county where they lived, and exchanged wedding vows, something they could not do in their home state. Virginia barred the two from marrying because Richard Loving was white and Mildred Jeter, whose ancestors were Cherokee Indian and African American, was considered "colored" under state law.

Richard Loving, a twenty-four-year-old bricklayer, and Mildred Jeter, eighteen, had grown up together in

Central Point. As a boy, Richard had spent many hours at Mildred's house listening to the music her seven brothers played. Although the U.S. Supreme Court had ruled in 1954 that public schools could not be segregated by race, none of the southern states had yet complied with the ruling. White and black children continued to attend separate schools, but they often played together and later worked together as young adults. Mildred soon attracted Richard's attention. The couple fell in love, and when Mildred became pregnant, they decided to marry.

Mildred did not know that Virginia banned marriages between blacks and whites, according to Phyl Newbeck, who interviewed her years later and wrote a book about the case, *Virginia Hasn't Always Been for Lovers*. She told Newbeck she believed they went to Washington, D.C., to get married because it would take less time and there was no blood test required there. Apparently Richard did know of the prohibition against interracial marriage in his home state. Neither of them, however, was aware that Virginia law made it a crime for couples to leave the state to marry and then return.

Police officials released Richard on bail after he spent one night in the county jail. Mildred, who was pregnant with the couple's first child, had to remain in jail for four days while she waited for the hearing on her case. She was not allowed to post bail.

GUILTY OF A FELONY
The young couple faced a felony charge punishable by up to five years in jail. According to Virginia law at that time, marriages between white and "colored" people were void. Those who did intermarry could be sentenced to confinement in the state penitentiary for "not less than one nor more than five years," as set forth in Section 20-59 of Virginia's Racial Integrity Statute. Section 20-58 of the

VIrGINIa coDe AGaInsT InTerracIaL MarrIaGe

Section 20-58 Leaving State to evade law. If any white person and colored person shall go out of the State, for the purpose of being married, and with the intention of returning, and be married out of it, and afterwards return to and reside in it, cohabiting as man and wife, they shall be punished as provided in Section 20-59, and the marriage shall be governed by the same law as if it had been solemnized in this State. The fact of their cohabitation here as man and wife shall be evidence of their marriage.

Section 20-59 Punishment for marriage. If any white person intermarry with a colored person, or any colored person intermarry with a white person, he shall be guilty of a felony and shall be punished by confinement in the penitentiary for not less than one nor more than five years.

same law stipulated that people who left the state to intermarry and returned to live as husband and wife faced the same felony penalty.

Richard and Mildred had separate hearings in the district court in Bowling Green, Virginia. Richard's case was heard on July 17, 1958, while Mildred had to appear in court on October 13. Both pleaded not guilty. During this time, the two had been forced to live apart, each staying with their parents.

Rejecting the not-guilty pleas for Mildred and Richard, Judge Edward Stehl III found probable cause for the felony charge against them and bound them over for trial before the grand jury. Following the advice of their lawyer, Frank Beazely, the two young people pled guilty, hoping the judge would have sympathy for their situation. By this time, Mildred had given birth to a baby boy. On January 6, 1959, however, Judge Leon M. Bazile found them guilty of a felony and sentenced each to a year in jail. He suspended the sentence provided they move from the state and live elsewhere for the next twenty-five years. Under the sentence, Mildred and Richard could visit the state but were not allowed to come to Virginia "together or at the same time."

After the judge issued the sentence, the Lovings moved to Washington, D.C., to live with Mildred's cousin. Richard commuted to Virginia, where he worked as a laborer. The banishment made life particularly difficult for Mildred, who returned home to Virginia for the births of two more children. Because of the court's ruling, Richard could not be with her.

"PLEASE HELP US IF YOU CAN"

Mildred Loving missed her country home, where she could walk down a tree-lined lane to get her mail and where children played on grassy lawns. "I was crying the blues all the time," she recalled years later.

While the Lovings lived in exile in Washington, D.C., and tended to their growing family, the push for black civil rights had reached a peak. In April and May of 1963, the Reverend Martin Luther King Jr. led an army of protesters—many of whom were children—in nonviolent marches in Birmingham, Alabama. Press coverage of police officers attacking the young protesters with fire hoses and dogs captured the nation's attention and mobilized politicians to take action. President John F. Kennedy announced his intention to ask Congress to pass a civil rights bill to end segregation. More than a year later,

THE REVEREND MARTIN LUTHER KING JR. LEADS PROTESTERS IN A MARCH ON
WASHINGTON (D.C.) FOR JOBS AND FREEDOM FOR BLACKS DURING THE CIVIL
RIGHTS CAMPAIGN. IT WAS AT THE MARCH THAT KING DELIVERED HIS ELO-
QUENT "I HAVE A DREAM" SPEECH, ON AUGUST 28, 1963, ON THE STEPS OF THE
LINCOLN MEMORIAL.

A SEVENTEEN-YEAR-OLD CIVIL RIGHTS DEMONSTRATOR, DEFYING AN ANTI-PARADE ORDINANCE IN BIRMINGHAM, ALABAMA, IS ATTACKED BY A POLICE DOG ON MAY 3, 1963. THIS PHOTOGRAPH APPEARED ON THE FRONT PAGE OF THE *NEW YORK TIMES* AND WAS DISCUSSED AT THE WHITE HOUSE THE FOLLOWING DAY DURING A MEETING ON THE CIVIL RIGHTS ISSUE.

Congress enacted the bill as the Civil Rights Act of 1964.

Mildred Loving's cousin suggested she write to Robert F. Kennedy, who as attorney general played a prominent role in the civil rights campaign. The cousin thought that Kennedy might be able to help lift the court order that kept the Lovings from moving back to Virginia. Kennedy advised the Lovings to contact the American Civil Liberties Union (ACLU), a national organization formed to protect individual freedom. In the preceding decade, ACLU attorneys had led the successful court battle to desegregate public schools in the landmark U.S. Supreme Court case, *Brown* v. *Board of Education*.

In her neat handwriting, on lined paper, Mildred Loving sent a plea for help to the ACLU in Washington, D.C. She explained the situation and the court order banishing the Lovings from their home state. "We know we can't live there," she wrote, "but we would like to go back once and awhile to visit our families and friends." She noted that she and her husband had three children and could not afford an attorney. "Please help us if you can. Hope to hear from you real soon," she concluded.

Mildred's note, written on June 20, 1963, set in motion a series of court battles that would eventually end in the highest court in the land—the U.S. Supreme Court.

WHAT MISCEGENATION IS !

—AND—

WHAT WE ARE TO EXPECT

Now that Mr. Lincoln is Re-elected.

By L. SEAMAN, LL. D.

WALLER & WILLETTS, Publishers,

NEW YORK.

A racist tract published during the Civil War played on whites' fears of interracial unions to incite opposition to President Abraham Lincoln's emancipation of the slaves.

TWO
LAWS AGAINST
INTERRACIAL MARRIAGE

THE UNION BETWEEN THE INDIAN PRINCESS
Pocahontas and the English colonist John Rolfe became
known as the first interracial marriage in North America.
Pocahontas (born Matoaka), the daughter of the Algon-
quian chief Powhatan, married Rolfe on April 5, 1614, at
Jamestown, Virginia. John Smith, captain of the colony,
later told how Pocahontas had prevented her father from
killing him during the early days of the settlement.
Whether such stories were true or not, colonists saw the
marriage as a way to cement friendly relationships
between the English colony and the native Indians.

As more Europeans settled in North America, liaisons
between whites and Indians increased. Several prominent
leaders of early America applauded such unions. Patrick
Henry, the firebrand patriot of the American Revolution,
suggested tax incentives and cash payments as a way to
encourage whites and Indians to marry. Thomas Jefferson
saw it as a way for Americans and Indians to "meet and
blend together, to intermix, and become one people."
However, Jefferson, Henry Clay, and for a time, Abraham
Lincoln all promoted the idea of deporting black
Americans as a way to solve racial problems and prevent
"mixing" between blacks and whites. Jefferson himself is

$150 REWARD

RANAWAY from the subscriber, on the night of the 2d instant, a negro man, who calls himself *Henry May*, about 22 years old, 5 feet 6 or 8 inches high, ordinary color, rather chunky built, bushy head, and has it divided mostly on one side, and keeps it very nicely combed; has been raised in the house, and is a first rate dining-room servant, and was in a tavern in Louisville for 18 months. I expect he is now in Louisville trying to make his escape to a free state, (in all probability to Cincinnati, Ohio.) Perhaps he may try to get employment on a steamboat. He is a good cook, and is handy in any capacity as a house servant. Had on when he left, a dark cassinett coatee, and dark striped cassinett pantaloons, new—he had other clothing. I will give $50 reward if taken in Louisvill; 100 dollars if taken one hundred miles from Louisville in this State, and 150 dollars if taken out of this State, and delivered to me, or secured in any jail so that I can get him again. WILLIAM BURKE.

Bardstown, Ky., September 3d, 1838.

AN 1838 FLYER OFFERS A REWARD FOR THE CAPTURE OF A RUNAWAY SLAVE NAMED HENRY MAY. TO MANY WHITE AMERICANS OF THE TIME, BLACKS WERE CONSIDERED PROPERTY, NOT HUMAN BEINGS.

generally acknowledged to have fathered children by his black slave, Sally Hemings, based on DNA testing done in 1998, and other evidence.

African slaves were first brought to North America aboard a Dutch ship in 1619. Over the next two centuries, the American colonists imported millions of captives from Africa to work on cotton, tobacco, and rice plantations in the South and on family farms and in households in the North. White indentured servants from poor families also served the wealthier merchants and farmers in

the colonies. Unions between these two groups of servants—married or not—produced a number of offspring of
mixed race.

Many whites in the colonies considered black people to
be inferior and sought ways to keep the two races separate.
Economics also played a role in unions between blacks and
whites. Children born of slave mothers and the white men
who ruled over them began appearing. Such couplings,
however, were largely ignored; the children, like their
mothers, were considered slaves. Most whites strongly
opposed marriages between blacks and whites, which
would have given mixed-race offspring legal standing as
citizens and threatened an economy based on slave labor.
In particular, white masters viewed unions between
white women and black men a threat to the "purity" of the
women and the white race.

Opposition to black-white relationships also came
from religious leaders. The Puritans believed the Bible
authorized slavery and viewed it as "punishment" for a
"miserable" race. They also opposed marriages between
what they considered "heathen" Africans and Christian
whites.

COLONIES PASS LAWS

In 1641 Massachusetts became the first American colony
to allow slavery. Laws against interracial marriage followed soon after. In 1661, Virginia passed the first ban on
interracial marriage. Those violating the ban had to pay a
fine of ten thousand pounds of tobacco. In the years that
followed, colonies increased the penalties for such relationships and punished the children of such unions as
well. In Maryland, a woman who married a slave also
became a slave.

In 1691, Virginia passed "An Act for Suppressing
Outlying Slaves." The act allowed local law officers to kill

or capture slaves who escaped from their masters. Under the legislation, slave owners whose runaway slaves were killed would receive 4,000 pounds of tobacco to compensate them for their loss. In addition, the law sought to prevent unions between blacks and whites and the children they might produce (described in the act as "that abominable mixture and spurious issue which hereafter may arise"). Such unions were labeled under various terms: amalgamation, miscegenation, and race mixing.

Under the law, white women with mixed-race children had to pay a fine of fifteen pounds to the church or become indentured servants for five years. (As a comparison, a saddle cost around two pounds in the 1700s, or almost $180 in 2000 money). Their children faced enforced servitude for thirty years. Whites who married blacks had to leave the state forever. The Virginia assembly revised the law in 1705 to include a six-month jail sentence plus fines on the white partner in an interracial marriage. Ministers who married such couples also had to pay a fine.

Despite such prohibitions, the number of children of parents of different races increased. In the late 1770s, at the time of the Revolutionary War, between 60,000 and 120,000 people of mixed race lived in North America. These included offspring of Indians and whites, blacks and whites, and Indians and blacks.

In the years leading up to the Civil War, states—particularly those that supported slavery—vigorously enforced the ban against blacks and whites marrying. In 1849, Virginia revised its code once more, this time to void all marriages between blacks and whites. On the other hand, the number of children with a black and a white parent continued to grow among the slave population. According to estimates, the number of mixed-race children increased by 67 percent between 1850 and 1860.

MISCEGENATION

The term miscegenation apparently came into use originally during the 1864 presidential election. Opponents of Abraham Lincoln circulated a pamphlet entitled "Miscegenation: The Theory of the Blending of the Races, Applied to the American White Man and Negro," claiming that Lincoln supported "race-mixing" or miscegenation (from the Latin words *miscere*, meaning to mix, and *genus*, or race). They hoped the charges would cause Lincoln, the Republican candidate, to lose the election. The plot failed when it became known that the publication had been produced by two Democrats, David Goodman Croly and George Wakeman.

PASSAGE OF THE FOURTEENTH AMENDMENT

Although the Civil War freed blacks from slavery, they remained a subjugated people. Radical Republicans intent on wresting control of the South from the wealthy plantation owners passed a series of bills to ensure rights for former slaves. The Freedmen's Bureau Bill, passed in 1865, protected the rights of blacks living in areas under federal control. A supplemental bill passed the next year guaranteed equal rights to all blacks. That same year, Congress passed a Civil Rights Act that granted citizenship to blacks. The bill also outlawed codes that discriminated against blacks in the South.

During debate on these bills, several senators

expressed concern that the legislation would override state laws against interracial marriage. Senator Thomas A. Hendricks of Indiana asked if the Civil Rights Act would repeal his state's antimiscegenation laws. "If the law of Indiana, as it does, prohibits under heavy penalty the marriage of a negro with a white woman," the senator asked, "may it be said a civil right is denied him which is enjoyed by all white men, to marry according to their choice?"

Senator Lyman Trumbull of Illinois, who sponsored the Civil Rights Act in the Senate, quickly assured his colleague that the bill would not interfere with states' marriage laws. He based his conclusion on the fact that such laws applied equally to both blacks and whites. "Are not both races treated alike by the law of Indiana?" he asked. "Does not the law make it just as much a crime for a white man to marry a black woman as for a black woman to marry a white man, and vice versa? I presume there is no discrimination in this respect, and therefore your law forbidding marriages between whites and blacks operates alike on both races."

The supplementary Freedmen's Bureau Bill passed in February 1866. Congress approved the Civil Rights Act the following month. President Andrew Johnson vetoed both bills. Congress overrode the vetoes, and both bills, with a few modifications, became law. It soon became obvious, however, that the bills would be repealed, either by the Supreme Court or the Congress, once a new administration won control. To prevent that, the Radical Republicans in Congress pushed for passage of a Fourteenth Amendment to the U.S. Constitution that would protect the rights of blacks.

The first section of the new amendment established that anyone born in the United States was a citizen. It guaranteed that states could not "abridge the privileges or immunities" of citizens; "deprive any person of life,

THE FOURTEENTH AMENDMENT: ENSURING RIGHTS FOR ALL

Section 1. All persons born or naturalized in the United States and subject to the jurisdiction thereof, are citizens of the United States and of the State wherein they reside. No State shall make or enforce any law which shall abridge the privileges or immunities of citizens of the United States; nor shall any State deprive any person of life, liberty, or property, without due process of law; nor deny to any person within its jurisdiction the equal protection of the laws.

The First Amendment bars the U.S. Congress from making any law that would establish a particular religion or prevent Americans from freely exercising their religion. It says nothing about what state legislatures can and cannot do.

For years the states used that loophole to pass laws that conflicted with First Amendment protections. In the 1845 case *Permoli* v. *Municipality No. 1 of City of New Orleans*, for example, the Supreme Court upheld the states' argument that the First Amendment did not apply to them. Justice John Catron, writing for the majority, ruled: "The Constitution makes no provision for protecting the citizens of the respective states in their religious liberties; this is left to the state constitutions and laws."

After the Civil War, Congress sought to close that particular loophole with the passage of the Fourteenth Amendment. Whites in the South had used the loophole to deprive freed slaves of their rights as citizens. With the ratification of the amendment on July 28, 1868, former slaves and all others "born or naturalized in the United States" automatically became American citizens. As citizens, they could vote, own property, and engage in business.

The amendment also directed the states not to deprive anyone, citizen and noncitizen alike, of "life, liberty, or property, without due process of law," or the "equal protection of the laws." In addition, the amendment specifically forbade the states from limiting citizens' "privileges or immunities."

For decades after the amendment was passed, however, it offered little protection against state actions. The *Slaughterhouse* cases set the stage for a conservative view of the amendment.

In March 1869 the Louisiana Legislature granted exclusive rights to the Crescent City Live-Stock Landing and Slaughter-House Company to run slaughterhouses in part of the state. Other slaughterhouse companies objected and filed suit. The U.S. Supreme Court heard the arguments in the suits—which became known as the *Slaughterhouse Cases*—in 1872 and 1873. The plaintiffs argued that the state had deprived them of their rights as citizens to earn a living, guaranteed under the Fourteenth Amendment. They also claimed the Louisiana law denied them "equal protection of the laws" and deprived them of liberty and property "without due process of law," in violation of the Fourteenth Amendment.

The Court ruled against the plaintiffs. In its April 14, 1873, decision, the Court decreed that the Fourteenth Amendment applied only to national rights. The amendment's protections did not extend to state contracts, state elections, or other matters overseen by the state, according to the Court. The ruling allowed states to control the civil rights of their citizens.

Over time, however, the Court began to apply the Fourteenth Amendment to protect citizens against wrongful actions by the states. Under this doctrine, the rights listed in the Bill of Rights are said to be *incorporated* by the Fourteenth Amendment. This doctrine has been referred to as "the second Bill of Rights" because it protected against unreasonable state power as the original ten amendments protected against federal abuses. Among other things, the policy played a key role in preserving Americans' religious liberties against state laws that favored certain religions.

One of the earliest cases in which the Court used the incorporation doctrine to limit a state's power was *Gitlow* v. *New York*. The case involved a socialist named Benjamin Gitlow, who was arrested after distributing copies of a paper urging people to strike and to take "revolutionary mass action." The state convicted Gitlow of advocating the overthrow of the government. In its decision, issued in 1925, the Court ruled against Gitlow because his actions endangered the state. Nevertheless, the Court asserted that the Fourteenth Amendment required states as well as Congress not to abridge the First Amendment's guarantee of free speech:

> [W]e may and do assume that freedom of speech and of the press—which are protected by the First Amendment from abridgment by Congress—are among the fundamental personal rights and "liberties" protected by the due process clause of the Fourteenth Amendment from impairment by the States.

In their dissent, Justices Oliver Wendell Holmes and Louis Brandeis argued that Gitlow's diatribe presented no immediate danger to the government and should be protected under the Constitution's free speech guarantees.

They, too, supported the doctrine that the Fourteenth Amendment protected free speech from state control.

During the 1930s and 1940s, the Supreme Court applied other First Amendment rights to the states. The Warren Court in the 1950s and 1960s made extensive use of the incorporation doctrine. With its focus on civil and individual rights, the Warren Court used the doctrine to order school desegregation, ban school prayers, and establish protections for criminal defendants. Later Courts have used the doctrine to strike down state laws banning abortion, guarantee privacy rights, and ensure other rights not specifically mentioned in the Constitution.

liberty, or property, without due process of law" [the due process clause]; or deny people "the equal protection of the laws" [the equal protection clause]. The amendment was ratified in 1868.

setbacks in court

During the next several decades, a series of U.S. Supreme Court rulings seriously limited the rights of black citizens covered by the Fourteenth Amendment. In an 1873 deci sion involving contracts awarded to slaughterhouses, the Court ruled that the Fourteenth Amendment did not apply to state contracts or a state's control over the civil rights of its citizens. Justice Stephen Field argued unsuccessfully that the amendment barred states from passing laws that interfered with the "privileges or immunities" of American citizens.

Congress passed another civil rights act in 1875 that guaranteed all Americans, regardless of race or color, "full and equal enjoyment" of buildings, inns, hired cabs, and other public spaces. But in 1883, the U.S. Supreme Court overturned the act. In its decision, the Court ruled that the Fourteenth Amendment did not apply to "social rights," such as equal access to facilities. Many believed interra cial marriage fell into the same category.

State courts upheld the view that marriage was the state's business. In an 1871 Indiana case, *State* v. *Gibson*, the state appeals court ruled that a law barring marriage between blacks and whites did not violate the Fourteenth Amendment or federal civil rights laws. The decision underscored the "inestimable importance" of the state's right "to regulate and control, to guard, protect, and pre serve this God-given, civilizing, and Christianizing insti tution [marriage]." Furthermore, the decision continued, the states could not "suffer or permit any interference" with the power to regulate marriage. The opinion noted that "divine" natural law barred interracial marriage and its result, "corruption of the races."

Using similar reasoning, an 1877 case in Alabama, *Green v. State*, upheld the right of the state to make marriages between blacks and whites a criminal offense.

In 1878, Virginia's state legislature made it illegal to leave the state with the intention of marrying someone of another race and then returning. The law also extended penalties to the black spouse in an interracial marriage for the first time. The penalty for such an act increased to two to five years in jail.

Virginia's laws on racial intermarriage met their first test that same year when the Virginia Supreme Court supported the state's public policy of banning such marriages. The decision, in *Kinney v. Commonwealth*, upheld the conviction of a white Virginia man who had been arrested for living with a woman, Mahala Miller, to whom he was not married. Like the Lovings, the couple had been legally married in Washington, D.C., but because Miller was black, Virginia law voided the marriage. In making the ruling, the state supreme court noted:

> The purity of public morals, the moral and physical development of both races, and the highest advancement of our cherished southern civilization . . . all require that they [black and white races] should be kept distinct and separate, and that connections and alliances so unnatural that God and nature seem to forbid them, should be prohibited by positive law, and be subject to no evasion.

The decision also firmly reiterated the rights of states to regulate marriage. The judge's words would be used in many following cases to reinforce that right:

There can be no doubt as to the power of every country to make laws regulating the marriage of its own subjects; to declare who may marry, how they may marry, and what shall be the legal consequences of their marrying. The right to regulate the institution of marriage; to classify the parties and persons who may lawfully marry; to dissolve the relation by divorce; and to impose such restraints upon the relation as the laws of God, and the laws of propriety, morality and social order demand, has been exercised by all civilized governments in all ages of the world.

In making the ruling, the court quoted a previous U.S. Supreme Court decision upholding the conviction of a man for marrying two wives. The 1878 bigamy case, *Reynolds* v. *United States*, reinforced the power of states to set their own laws on marriage. "It is impossible to believe that the constitutional guaranty of religious freedom was intended to prohibit legislation in respect to this most important feature of social life," wrote Chief Justice Morrison R. Waite in his majority opinion.

Another U. S. Supreme Court ruling, in *Pace* v. *Alabama*, decided in 1883, determined that laws based on race were constitutional as long as penalties were the same for people of all races. The opinion upheld the conviction of a black man for living with a white woman. The man claimed that the Alabama law violated the Fourteenth Amendment, which guaranteed equal protection of the laws. In turning down his plea, the Supreme Court noted that "the punishment of each offending person, whether white or black, is the same." Therefore, the Court ruled, the law met the Constitution's requirement of "equal protection."

"RACIAL INTEGRITY"

Black Americans were not the only ones to endure racial discrimination. As the Industrial Revolution took hold in the late 1800s and early 1900s, immigrants from around the world came to America searching for jobs and a better life. In many regions, already established inhabitants resented the newcomers and feared they would take away jobs and overrun their communities. Noted Americans such as Samuel Morse (inventor of the telegraph) and President Theodore Roosevelt supported measures to bar certain immigrants or to deny them citizenship. In the West, hate groups incited fears against a "yellow peril," aimed at the work crews from China, and later Japan, brought to the United States to work on the railroads in the late 1880s. Poor blacks and whites migrated to cities, where they lived and worked in close proximity. This heightened fears of "race mixing." The Ku Klux Klan, a violent white supremacist group, donned white sheets and terrorized blacks, Jews, and Catholics in towns in the South and North. Many whites who traced their heritage back to England considered people from Ireland, Italy, Poland, and Eastern European nations to be from inferior races different from their own.

During this time, too, white supremacists embraced the newly introduced field of eugenics. Studies of animal breeding had revealed that certain traits were passed from parent to offspring. Adapted to humans, these studies played into the hands of those arguing for preserving the "purity" of the white race. Since they believed that the white (or Anglo-Saxon) race was superior, these proponents of eugenics argued that the inferior traits of other races would "weaken" the children of interracial parents. The children, in turn, would pass along the "weak" traits to their own offspring. People warned against the "mongrelization of the white race" and "race

DEFINING RACE

One problem the states encountered in enforcing antimiscegenation laws was defining exactly who was black and who was white. Logically, a person born of interracial parents would be half one race and half the other. But in the case of blacks, economics and racism outweighed logic. White slave owners had a strong incentive to classify people with any trace of African heritage as black in order to retain them as slaves.

Under Virginia law until 1910, anyone with 25 percent or more of African blood was classified as black. In 1910 lawmakers changed the percentage to 15 percent, and in 1924, with the passage of the Racial Integrity Act of 1924, the "one-drop" measure became law.

Whites who considered blacks inferior had long argued that even a drop of African blood would "pollute" the "pure" white race. In 1900, the black leader and educator Booker T. Washington—son of a white father and a black mother—commented on this view: "If a person is known to have one percent of African blood in his veins, he ceases to be a white man. The ninety-nine percent of Caucasian blood . . . counts for nothing. The person is a Negro every time."

The harsh treatment of blacks in the South and elsewhere induced some offspring of interracial parents to try to "pass" as white. When couples applied for a marriage license, local clerks had the responsibility of determining who had a "drop" of African blood and who could be classified as having "no trace whatsoever of any blood other than Caucasian."

suicide." Later research would disprove these theories, but the concept resonated with a public already fearful of those different from themselves.

Responding to these fears, the Virginia legislature in 1924 introduced an act titled "A Bill to Preserve the Integrity of the White Race." Later passed as the Racial Integrity Act of 1924, the legislation comprised ten codes aimed at preventing interracial marriage. It retained previous restrictions against the marriage of blacks and whites, but expanded the ban to include Asians and other nonwhite races. The most sweeping change was the definition of a white person as one "who has no trace whatsoever of any blood other than Caucasian."

Whites, under the law, could marry only other whites. The legislators made one exception, apparently in recognition of Pocahontas's supposed role in sparing the lives of Jamestown colonists. The law provided that people who had "one-sixteenth or less of the blood of the American Indian and no other non-Caucasic blood" would be considered to be white.

Other states adopted similar bans. Several Western states made it illegal for whites to marry Asians or American Indians. On the national level, Congress banned all Chinese workers from immigrating to the United States in 1882. Chinese people already in the country were not allowed to become citizens. The Immigration Act adopted by Congress in 1924 limited the number of immigrants from southern and eastern Europe and barred most immigrants from Japan.

THree
CAMPAIGN FOR CIVIL RIGHTS

DESPITE THE CONSTITUTION'S GUARANTEES, blacks continued to be victims of discrimination. In most of the South and many areas of the North, blacks could not stay in hotels open to whites. They were barred from restaurants, restrooms, swimming pools, and other public facilities where whites gathered. They had to use separate drinking fountains and ride in the back of public buses. Throughout the South, signs designated "white only" and "colored only" areas. In seventeen states, laws required black and white students to attend separate schools. Four other states and the District of Columbia allowed local school boards to separate students by race. Although proponents of the system claimed they ran "separate but equal" schools for students of both races, in most cases schools for blacks were markedly inferior to those for whites.

In 1954, the U.S. Supreme Court under Chief Justice Earl Warren ruled that segregated schools violated black children's constitutional rights. The unanimous decision, *Brown* v. *Board of Education*, based on the Fourteenth Amendment's guarantee of equal protection, required states to desegregate schools. Lawyers opposed to desegregation had argued that the framers of the Fourteenth Amendment had never intended to intrude on states'

LINDA BROWN, LEFT, WITH HER SISTER, TERRY, AND PARENTS, LEOLA AND OLIVER, STAND OUTSIDE THEIR KANSAS HOME IN 1953. LINDA'S FATHER FILED A SUIT ON HIS DAUGHTER'S BEHALF AGAINST THE TOPEKA, KANSAS, BOARD OF EDUCATION AFTER THE BOARD REFUSED TO ALLOW LINDA TO ATTEND THE CITY'S ALL-WHITE SCHOOL. THAT SCHOOL WAS CLOSER TO THE BROWNS' HOME AND HAD BETTER FACILITIES THAN THE SCHOOLS FOR BLACK STUDENTS. THE FOLLOWING YEAR, THE U.S. SUPREME COURT RULED IN LINDA'S FAVOR, STRIKING DOWN SEGREGATION IN THE NATION'S SCHOOLS.

rights to determine how to educate their children. Chief Justice Warren, however, said that the Court's study of the amendment's history had proved to be "inconclusive." The Court, he noted, had decided it could not base its opinion on conditions that existed in 1868, when the amendment was adopted.

The following year, the Court again ruled against racial discrimination in public education and ordered states to desegregate schools "with all deliberate speed." The ruling marked the beginning of a long, bitter battle over desegregation. White parents held violent demonstrations against the policy. Among their main concerns, many said, was that joint schooling would lead to interracial relationships and marriages. One critic of the *Brown* decision, Mississippi Circuit Judge Tom P. Brady, commented on this fear:

> You cannot place little white and Negro children in classrooms and not have integration. They will sing together, dance together, eat together, and play together. They will grow up together and the sensitivity of the white children will be dulled. Constantly the Negro will be endeavoring to usurp every right and privilege which will lead to intermarriage.

ADVANCES IN CIVIL RIGHTS

Schools were not the only arena in which blacks fought for equal rights. On December 1, 1955, a black housekeeper and seamstress named Rosa Parks refused a bus driver's command to go to the back of the bus in Montgomery, Alabama. Her act of defiance led to a citywide bus boycott and spearheaded a national campaign for black civil rights. The Reverend Martin Luther King Jr., a Montgomery minister, led the yearlong bus boycott. Its success catapulted the charismatic King to leadership of a nationwide effort to win rights for black Americans.

Violence against blacks escalated as the push for black civil rights gathered strength. Sexual relations between blacks and whites particularly enraged white supremacists. Merely looking at a white woman could get a black man lynched. In 1955, a mob of white supremacists in Mississippi brutally murdered a fourteen-year-old boy named Emmett Till after he allegedly whistled at a white woman. The boy, from Chicago, had been visiting relatives. Anguished and enraged over her son's death, Emmett's mother, Mamie Till, ordered an open casket at the funeral, which allowed the Northern press to publish photographs of Emmett's mutilated body. The gruesome pictures disgusted many and added to the chorus of voices demanding civil rights for black Americans.

In 1958, the year Richard Perry Loving and Mildred Jeter Loving married, bombings in black schools and churches in the South led President Dwight D. Eisenhower to introduce a civil rights bill. Passed in 1960, it was the first legislation in almost a century to protect black voting rights. The law had little success since local juries often sympathized with violators, but it did begin the push in Congress to deal with the issue of equal rights for blacks. Under the leadership of President Lyndon Johnson and Attorney General Robert F. Kennedy, Congress passed the Civil Rights Act of 1964. A much stronger law, the act banned racial discrimination and put enforcement in the hands of federal authorities. The Voting Rights Act of 1965, which required states to lift restrictions that prevented blacks from voting, won Congressional approval the following year.

During this time, gains had also been made in easing restrictions against interracial marriage. At one time, forty states (including the territories of Kansas, New Mexico, and Washington) barred blacks from marrying whites. Northern states began repealing laws against interracial marriage as early as 1780, when Pennsylvania lifted its ban. Massachusetts, pressured by antislavery activists, followed suit nearly sixty years later. Abolitionists William Lloyd Garrison and Lewis Tappan argued for intermarriage among the races as a way to reduce racial tensions and "break down those petty distinctions which are the effect of climate or locality of situation, and which lead to oppression, war, and division among mankind."

After the Civil War, several other states repealed restrictions on interracial marriages. By the turn of the century, antimiscegenation laws remained on the books in thirty states. The situation remained unchanged until the 1950s, when eight more states rescinded laws against interracial marriage. World War II had given Americans a view of the horrors of the Nazi regime and its attack on civil liberties, including laws banning marriages between white "Aryans" and Jews. After the war, the United Nations issued a Universal Declaration of Human Rights, which the United States signed in 1948. Among the human rights listed in the declaration was the right to marry "without any limitation due to race."

With growing support for the civil rights campaign, several states, most in the West, reexamined their anti-miscegenation laws. By the late 1960s, when the *Loving* case was heard, only sixteen states—all in Southern states and states bordering the South—still retained the laws (Maryland repealed its law just before oral arguments in the case). All sixteen antimiscegenation codes had been upheld either by lower courts or the state courts of appeal.

COURT-ORDERED REPEAL

For almost a century, the U.S. Supreme Court and the state courts had validated antimiscegenation laws. One such decision, in a 1932 case, *Wood* v. *Commonwealth*, reconfirmed that in Virginia, "the preservation of racial integrity is the unquestioned policy of this State, and that it is sound and wholesome."

California's highest court became the first to overturn state laws against interracial marriage, in the 1948 case *Perez* v. *Sharp*. The case involved a white woman, Andrea Perez, and a black man, Sylvester Davis, who had been denied a marriage license. At the time, California law prohibited marriages between whites and spouses who were "Negro, mulatto, Mongolian or member of the Malay race." The state had no similar ban against interracial sex or on interracial marriages that had taken place beyond state borders.

The couple sued, claiming that the state's ban on interracial marriage denied them the right to practice their religion guaranteed under the First Amendment. They contended that their religion, Catholicism, encouraged marriage without any limits regarding race. When the lower court rejected their plea, the couple appealed to the California Supreme Court.

In a close 4 to 3 decision, the court discarded the First Amendment argument but upheld the appeal based on constitutional guarantees of equal protection and due process. Striking down California's antimiscegenation law, the court's opinion held that marriage was a "fundamental right of free men" that states could not infringe upon without "an important social objective and by reasonable means." The state had not met that requirement, according to the court. Justice Roger J. Traynor, writing for the majority, dismissed the state's contention that a ban on interracial marriage was necessary to prevent the birth of unhealthy, inferior offspring. "Experts are agreed that the progeny of marriages between persons of different races are not inferior to both parents," Traynor noted.

He similarly rejected the argument that such laws were needed to protect offspring of interracial parents who would suffer psychological damage. "If they do, the fault lies not with their parents, but with the prejudices in the community and the laws that perpetuate those prejudices by giving legal force to the belief that certain races are inferior," the justice wrote.

Furthermore, Traynor noted, the laws could not be justified by fears that their repeal would lead to racial strife. "It is no answer to say that race tension can be eradicated through the perpetuation by law of the prejudices that give rise to the tension," he asserted.

Traynor concluded that race was not a valid justification for the ban or for overriding citizens' rights. "By restricting the individual's right to marry on the basis of race alone, they violate the equal protection of the laws clause of the United States Constitution."

Following the *Perez* ruling, courts in two other states, Nevada in 1958 and Arizona in 1959, struck down antimiscegenation laws in those regions.

supreme court review

An Alabama case presented the opportunity for the high court to review interracial marriage laws in 1954. In that case, a black woman, Linnie Jackson, had become involved sexually with a white man, A. C. Burcham. Even though Burcham was married to someone else, the state charged the couple with violating Alabama's ban on interracial marriage. Jackson's attorney's argument that the code was unconstitutional did not sway the court, which found Jackson guilty and sentenced her to two years in jail. She appealed. The appeals court denied her claim and upheld the sentence. In affirming the lower court's decision, the court of appeals ruled that the state had the right to set regulations "as the laws of God and the laws of propriety, morality and social order demand."

When the state supreme court denied Jackson's request to review the lower courts' rulings, her lawyer petitioned for a hearing before the U.S. Supreme Court. The Court turned down the request at Justice Felix Frankfurter's urging. Three justices—Chief Justice Earl Warren and Justices William O. Douglas and Hugo L. Black—voted to hear the case, but they did not prevail. Just months earlier, the Court had delivered its decision in *Brown* v. *Board of Education* on May 17, 1954, prohibiting segregation in the nation's public schools. Embroiled as they were in the furor over the school desegregation cases, the justices wanted to avoid arousing Southern sentiment further by turning the spotlight on interracial marriage.

The Court turned down another chance to decide the issue a year later when it rejected an Asian man's request for an appeal. In 1955, the Virginia Supreme Court ruled on an interracial marriage involving a white woman and an Asian man in *Naim* v. *Naim*. As in the *Loving* case, the couple had left Virginia to be married and then returned to the state. The Virginia Supreme Court agreed with the white spouse (and the state) that the marriage should be considered void. The court's decision reaffirmed the state's right to regulate marriage. "The institution of marriage," the opinion read, "has from time immemorial been considered a proper subject for State regulation in the interest of the public health, morals and welfare." Furthermore, the ruling delivered yet another blow to the argument, supported by *Perez*, that the Fourteenth Amendment protected interracial couples. The amendment, according to the unanimous opinion, contained "no requirement that the State shall not legislate to prevent the obliteration of racial pride but must permit the corruption of blood even though it weaken and destroy the quality of its citizenship."

RICHARD AND MILDRED LOVING REVIEW THEIR COURT CASE WITH THEIR LAWYER IN MAY 1965 AS THEIR DAUGHTER PEGGY WAITS TO GO HOME.

The U.S. Supreme Court denied Naim's request for a hearing and sent the case back to state court for a retrial. The Virginia Supreme Court ignored the order and dismissed the case, leaving the judgment intact. The U.S. Supreme Court did not pursue the matter further. Just as in the *Jackson* case, it was suspected that the Court was reluctant to further enrage Southerners by opening discussion on interracial marriage. The issue would have to wait for another day.

Less than a year after Mildred Loving appealed to the

ACLU for help, the civil rights organization successfully defended another couple before the Supreme Court. The case, *McLaughlin* v. *Florida*, involved a state law that barred unmarried interracial couples from living and sleeping together on a regular basis. The state had no such ban on the same behavior by couples of the same race. Florida's code prohibited adultery and sex between unmarried people. Under the law, officials had to provide proof that couples of the same race had had sexual intercourse before obtaining a conviction. If a black person and a white person were charged with the offense, however, no proof of intercourse was required.

In 1961, Florida officials charged a black man, Dewey McLaughlin, and a white woman, Connie Hoffman, with violating the state's ban on interracial cohabitation. The two were arrested after Hoffman's landlady reported to police that she had seen McLaughlin in the woman's apartment. After a trial in state court, a jury found the couple guilty and they were sentenced to thirty days in jail and fined $150. Arguing that the law violated their clients' Fourteenth Amendment right to equal protection, the couple's lawyers appealed the convictions to the state supreme court. They contended the law treated McLaughlin and Hoffman more harshly because they were of different races than if they had been of the same race.

After the Florida Supreme Court rejected the couple's plea, the case went before the U.S. Supreme Court. In December 1964, Justice Byron White delivered the Court's unanimous decision to strike down the Florida law. The more stringent code, because it applied only to interracial couples, denied McLaughlin and Hoffman "the equal protection of the laws guaranteed by the Fourteenth Amendment," the Court ruled. In doing so, it dismissed the reasoning in the earlier *Pace* v. *Alabama* that justified laws based on race if the penalties were equal for both races. "This narrow view of the Equal Protection Clause was soon swept away," White wrote in *McLaughlin*.

In deciding whether a law met constitutional requirements, the opinion noted, the Court had to determine that the purpose behind the law was reasonable. In the *McLaughlin* case, White said, that meant checking to see if there was "an arbitrary or invidious discrimination between those [groups] covered by Florida's cohabitation law and those excluded." The Court's investigation revealed that Florida had no valid reason to treat interracial couples differently. "We find nothing . . . which makes it essential to punish promiscuity of one racial group and not that of another," White concluded.

Florida had argued that its laws against interracial marriage justified different standards for interracial couples. The Court rejected that argument. However, the opinion did not rule on the state's antimiscegenation laws or on the state's claim that history showed that the Fourteenth Amendment did not apply to such laws.

In a brief concurrence joined by Justice Douglas, Justice Potter Stewart rejected altogether the claim that the Constitution would ever allow state laws that base criminal behavior on a person's race. "These appellants were convicted, fined, and imprisoned under a statute which made their conduct criminal only because they were of different races," he noted. "Discrimination of that kind is invidious per se."

MILDRED AND RICHARD LOVING SHARE LAUGHS WITH FRIENDS IN MAY 1965.
AT THE TIME, AUTHORITIES HAD ALLOWED THEM TO MOVE BACK TO VIRGINIA
WHILE THEY WAITED FOR THE VIRGINIA SUPREME COURT OF APPEALS TO
DECIDE THEIR CASE.

four
BACK IN COURT

MILDreD LOVInG'S LeTTer asking for help arrived at the offices of the Washington, D.C., branch of the American Civil Liberties Union while *McLaughlin* was in the works but before it had been argued before the Supreme Court. Officials there referred the case to Bernard S. Cohen, one of the young lawyers who founded the local ACLU branch and was a volunteer with the organization.

Cohen met with the Lovings and agreed to represent them. The ACLU had been searching for cases to challenge the antimiscegenation statutes, which civil libertarians considered a relic of slavery days. The organization believed the Loving case would fit the bill.

Cohen had a long way to go, however, before presenting the case to the U.S. Supreme Court. The first step required him to get the case back into Judge Leon Maurice Bazile's courtroom. It had been four years since the judge had issued his ruling in the *Loving* case, and Virginia law required defendants to appeal their convictions within 120 days. Extensive research led the lawyer to conclude that the Lovings' case had never been completely dismissed by the court, since the couple had been given a suspended sentence that could be reimposed if they violated the conditions.

The judge allowed Cohen to file a motion on the case. On November 6, 1963, the lawyer asked the court to dismiss the charges against the Lovings. He argued that the state's antimiscegenation laws were unconstitutional, that the laws denied the Lovings equal protection of the law and the "fundamental right" of marriage, and that the court's order that the Lovings leave the state violated their right to due process of law.

Several months went by, and Judge Bazile did not rule on the motion. Cohen sought the advice of his former law school professor, Chet Antieu, at Georgetown University. While there, Cohen met another former student, Philip J. Hirschkop, who specialized in civil rights law. Hirschkop offered to help Cohen with the *Loving* appeal. Eventually, Hirschkop joined Cohen's law firm and the two spent the next three years working on the case together. In addition to both being Georgetown alumni, Cohen and Hirschkop shared a common background. They both had grown up in Brooklyn, New York, in Jewish families. Early in their careers, they had become involved in civil rights issues, Cohen as a volunteer lawyer for the ACLU and Hirschkop as a young assistant to famed civil rights attorney William Kunstler.

When Judge Bazile still did not respond to requests to rule on Cohen's motion, the Lovings' lawyers filed a motion in federal court on October 28, 1964, asking judges there to address the matter. Almost a year after the original filing, a three-judge panel directed the state to issue a ruling on the motion or the case would be moved to federal court.

By this time, the U.S. Supreme Court had ruled on the *McLaughlin* case, striking down Florida's interracial cohabitation law, but leaving untouched the state's interracial marriage code. Also during this period, Mildred and Richard Loving returned home to Virginia after

PHILIP J. HIRSCHKOP, ONE OF THE LAWYERS REPRESENTING THE LOVINGS IN
THEIR SUPREME COURT CASE, FIRST BECAME INVOLVED IN THE CAMPAIGN FOR
RACIAL EQUALITY WHILE SERVING AS AN ASSISTANT TO NOTED CIVIL RIGHTS
LAWYER WILLIAM KUNSTLER, PICTURED ABOVE.

almost six years of exile. An order issued by the three-
judge panel allowed the couple to live together in King and
Queen County (next to Caroline County, the site of their
hometown), Virginia, while the case made its way through
the legal system. As officials in the state government
raged, the Lovings' neighbors in the racially mixed community where they resided accepted them without problems. The couple lived quietly in their new home, with no
incidents of violence reported and no demonstrations.

As the case progressed, however, the lawyers who took on their cause became targets of outraged racists. Some fellow lawyers ignored them. Vandals disabled their cars by filling the gas tanks with sugar. They received threatening telephone calls and were referred to as "two Jew lawyers" in racist newspaper articles.

A RULING AND AN APPEAL

Finally, Judge Bazile filed his opinion and on January 22, 1965, issued an order denying Cohen's motion. The judge rejected the claim that Virginia's laws violated the Constitution, stating that "there is nothing in . . . the Fourteenth Amendment which has anything to do with this subject here under consideration." Citing a number of court cases from the 1800s to support his views, Judge Bazile said that the Lovings' sentence should not be considered cruel and unusual. That term, he contended, applied only to punishments involving "burning at the stake, crucifixion, breaking on the wheel or the like."

In giving the reasons for his ruling, Judge Bazile concluded, "Almighty God created the races white, black, yellow, Malay and red, and He placed them on separate continents, and but for the interference with His arrangement there would be no cause for such marriages. The fact that he separated the races shows that he did not intend for the races to mix."

Cohen and Hirschkop appealed the judge's ruling, asking that the case be heard in federal court. Instead, the case moved to the Supreme Court of Appeals of Virginia. Denying the Lovings' appeal, the appeals court noted that none of the court cases cited by the couple's attorneys "deals with miscegenation statutes or curtails a legal truth which has always been recognized—that there is an overriding state interest in the institution of marriage." The state's interracial marriage laws, according to the appeals court, did not violate the Constitution. The court went on to say that it saw "no sound judicial reason" to issue a ruling that would conflict with the *Naim* decision, which the *Loving* attorneys had asked the court to overturn. More than ten years had passed since the *Naim* decision had been issued, the court said, and no other cases had challenged its conclusions (that the Constitution did not prevent the state from regulating marriage).

In January 1965, Virginia Circuit Court Judge Leon M. Bazile turned down the Lovings' request to dismiss the charges against them. In issuing his ruling, the judge lectured that God had separated the races and did not want them to mix.

NEXT STOP: THE SUPREME COURT

The appeals court decision, issued in March 1966, had been expected. Cohen and Hirschkop knew the next step would be an appeal to the U. S. Supreme Court. The *McLaughlin* case helped set the stage for the appeal. Although the Supreme Court had declined to rule on interracial marriage statutes in the earlier case, the *Loving* lawyers believed the Court would not avoid the issue when presented with a case like their clients' that was so directly affected by the ban. The case would allow the ACLU to push the Supreme Court to finally make a ruling on the statutes. And given the Court's rulings on *Brown*, *McLaughlin*, and other landmark cases that had struck down state laws that infringed on individual rights, they were hopeful that the Court would view interracial marriage in the same light.

THROUGH THE COURT SYSTEM

First Stop: State Court
Almost all cases (about 95 percent) start in state courts.
These courts go by various names, depending on the state
in which they operate: circuit, district, municipal, county,
or superior. The case is tried and decided by a judge, a
panel of judges, or a jury.

The side that loses can then appeal to the next level.

First Stop: Federal Court
U.S. DISTRICT COURT—About 5 percent of cases begin
their journey in federal court. Most of these cases concern
federal laws, the U.S. Constitution, or disputes that
involve two or more states. They are heard in one of the
ninety-four U.S. district courts in the nation.
U.S. COURT OF INTERNATIONAL TRADE—Federal court
cases involving international trade appear in the U.S.
Court of International Trade.
U.S. COURT OF FEDERAL CLAIMS—The U.S. Court of
Federal Claims hears federal cases that involve more than
$10,000, Indian claims, and some disputes with govern-
ment contractors.

The loser in federal court can appeal to the next level.

Appeals: State Cases
Forty states have appeals courts that hear cases that have
come from the state courts. In states without an appeals
court, the case goes directly to the state supreme court.

Appeals: Federal Cases
U.S. CIRCUIT COURT—Cases appealed from U.S. district
courts go to U.S. circuit courts of appeals. There are twelve
circuit courts that handle cases from throughout the
nation. Each district court and every state and territory

are assigned to one of the twelve circuits. Appeals in a few state cases—those that deal with rights guaranteed by the U.S. Constitution—are also heard in this court.

U.S. COURT OF APPEALS—Cases appealed from the U.S. Court of International Trade and the U.S. Court of Federal Claims are heard by the U.S. Court of Appeals for the Federal Circuit. Among the cases heard in this court are those involving patents and minor claims against the fed eral government.

Further Appeals: State Supreme Court

Cases appealed from state appeals courts go to the highest courts in the state—usually called supreme courts. In New York, the state's highest court is called the court of appeals. Most state cases do not go beyond this point.

Final Appeals: U.S. Supreme Court

The U.S. Supreme Court is the highest court in the country. Its decision on a case is the final word. The Court decides issues that can affect every person in the nation. It has decided cases on slavery, abortion, school segregation, and many other important issues.

The Court selects the cases it will hear—usually around one hundred each year. Four of the nine justices must vote to consider a case in order for it to be heard. Almost all cases have been appealed from the lower courts (either state or federal).

Most people seeking a decision from the Court submit a petition for *certiorari*. Certiorari means that the case will be moved from a lower court to a higher court for review. The Court receives about nine thousand of these requests annually. The petition outlines the case and gives reasons why the Court should review it.

In rare cases, for example *New York Times* v. *United States*, an issue must be decided immediately. When such a case is of national importance, the Court allows it to bypass the usual lower court system and hears the case directly.

To win a spot on the Court's docket, a case must fall within one of the following categories:

· Disputes between states and the federal government or between two or more states. The Court also reviews cases involving ambassadors, consuls, and foreign ministers.

· Appeals from state courts that have ruled on a federal question.

· Appeals from federal appeals courts (about two-thirds of all requests fall into this category).

The lawyers still had hurdles to clear, however, before the case reached the Supreme Court. First, they had to convince the Court to review it. Each year, thousands of people petition the Court for a hearing. That number has increased rapidly. During the 1960 term, for example, lawyers submitted 2,313 cases for review. In 2006, justices had a caseload of about 9,000. Only about one hundred cases are selected for a hearing during the term.

Justices review potential cases behind the closed doors of their chambers. The chief justice or an associate justice presents the cases they believe should come before the Court. A discussion may follow on the merits or drawbacks to hearing the case. In order to win a spot on the schedule, a case must have the vote of at least four justices.

Cases come to the Supreme Court through two routes: a petition for *certiorari* or on appeal. Most cases follow the *certiorari* route. A *certiorari* petition is a formal request that the case be moved from a lower court to a higher court. *Certiorari* means "to be informed of." If the petition is granted, the record of the previous hearing or trial is then sent to the higher court for review (so the court will be "informed" of the proceedings). Lawyers include on the petition the facts of the case and the reasons it should be heard. The *Loving* case followed the less common route of appeal. When appealing a case from a state court, as in the *Loving* case, lawyers must prove that a federal or constitutional question is at stake. They present the questions raised and the reasons why the Court should get involved in the case in a jurisdictional statement filed with the Court.

If the Court does agree to hear the case, lawyers on both sides must organize their arguments in a brief, which the justices will use to help them decide the outcome. Each brief outlines the facts of the case, the lower courts' rulings, and detailed arguments to support one side of the question or the other. Courts rely on previous decisions when forming their opinions, so lawyers cite as many cases as they can to bolster their arguments.

The Court schedules oral arguments to be conducted several months after the submission of the briefs. During these open sessions, the nine robed justices listen to each side present his or her case. Often justices interrupt the presentation to ask questions or make comments. Sometimes the Court allows a supporter of one side or the other (called *amicus curiae* or "friend of the court") to make a case as well. The justices then retreat to their chambers, where they discuss the case in private and ultimately vote on the final decision. Justices who agree with the majority but want to add their own reasons for doing so can write a concurrence. Those who disagree with the majority opinion can write a dissent. The majority decision becomes the law of the land upon which future opinions will rely. But brilliantly worded dissents can sometimes lead the way to overturning a decision that a later Court can no longer support.

After being notified of the state appeals court's ruling, Cohen and Hirschkop filed a notice of appeal with the U.S. Supreme Court. On July 29, 1966, the two lawyers submitted a jurisdictional statement supporting their appeal. Two prominent ACLU lawyers, Melvin L. Wulf and David Carliner, assisted in preparing the statement and later, the brief. Wulf was the national legal director for the ACLU, and Carliner had been lead ACLU attorney on the *Naim* case.

In the twenty-page statement, the lawyers argued that the U.S. Supreme Court had jurisdiction in the case and that it presented "substantial federal questions." The lawyers purposefully referred to all ten sections of Virginia's antimiscegenation code, even though the Lovings had been charged under only two sections, 20-58 and 20-59. It was their aim to convince the Court to review the entire code and, they hoped, reject it all. In addition, the statement spelled out three of the sections: 20-58, the prohibition against interracial couples leaving the state to marry and then returning; 20-59, the punishment for interracial marriage; and 20-54, which spelled out the meaning of "white person" and the requirement that whites marry only whites.

The lawyers made three arguments, citing the Court's decisions in *Brown* and *McLaughlin* among others:

· All of the statutes were "racially discriminatory" and denied the Lovings "as individuals, and Negroes and whites as groups, the equal protection of the laws."

· The state, by not allowing the Lovings to marry, denied the Lovings due process of law.

· The antimiscegenation laws violated federal codes that guarantee everyone "the full and equal benefit of all laws."

The statement concluded with a summary of how the laws had disrupted the lives of the Lovings and others like them. Because of the ban, the Lovings could not live in their hometown and raise their children there. Their children were labeled as bastards because the laws voided the Lovings' marriage. The Lovings could not collect Social Security or other benefits to which other married couples were entitled. Their children would not automatically inherit their assets.

The Supreme Court of Appeals of Virginia wrongly decided that the state laws were constitutional, the lawyers argued. They asked the U.S. Supreme Court to review the

VIRGINIA'S DEFINITION OF RACES

Section 20-54 Intermarriage prohibited; meaning of term "white persons."—It shall hereafter be unlawful for any white person in this State to marry any save a white person, or a person with no other admixture of blood than white and American Indian. For the purpose of this chapter, the term "white person" shall apply only to such person as has no trace whatever of any blood other than Caucasian; but persons who have one-sixteenth or less of the blood of the American Indian and have no other non-Caucasic blood shall be deemed to be white persons. All laws heretofore passed and now in effect regarding the intermarriage of white and colored persons shall apply to marriages prohibited by this chapter.

Va. Code Ann. 1-14 Colored persons and Indians defined.—Every person in whom there is ascertainable any Negro blood shall be deemed and taken to be a colored person, and every person not a colored person having one fourth or more of American Indian blood shall be deemed an American Indian; except that members of Indian tribes existing in this Commonwealth having one fourth or more of Indian blood and less than one sixteenth of Negro blood shall be deemed tribal Indians."

case and to reverse the lower court's judgment in favor of the Lovings.

THE STATE REPLIES

As was customary, the Court's clerk requested Virginia's attorney general to respond to the Lovings' appeal. The state of Virginia filed a twenty-three-page reply on November 18, 1966, asking the Court not to consider the case. State Attorney General Robert Y. Button and two assistant attorneys general, Kenneth C. Patty and Robert D. McIlwaine III, prepared the document. McIlwaine had helped write an *amicus* brief in the *Naim* case, defending the state's antimiscegenation laws.

In the reply to the Lovings' appeal, the state based its objections on three points:

- Sections 58 and 59 of the Virginia antimiscegenation code did not violate the Fourteenth Amendment.

- The framers of the amendment never intended for that document to interfere with the states' right to regulate marriage.

- Numerous decisions by both state and federal courts upheld that view.

Noting the overwhelming number of conflicting treatises on the subject, the statement concluded that state legislatures, not the Court, should weigh the evidence and determine how best to regulate interracial marriage. The state's lawyers urged the Court not even to consider statutes other than Sections 58 and 59 of the Virginia code. Those two statutes, the state pointed out, were the only laws under which the Lovings had been charged.

The question on which the Lovings based their appeal—whether the Virginia code violated the Constitution—was "so unsubstantial," the state said, that the Supreme Court had no business considering the case.

On December 12, 1966, the U.S. Supreme Court announced that it would hear the *Loving* case. Oral arguments on the matter were scheduled for April 10, 1967. Months of hard work lay before the lawyers on both sides as they began the arduous task of writing briefs and preparing for oral arguments that would convince the nation's highest court that their views should prevail.

FIVE
MAKING THEIR CASE

Preparing Briefs for a U.S. Supreme Court case may be the most difficult job a lawyer faces. Not only does the task demand months of research; it also requires a skillful writer with the ability to organize all the facts and shape arguments so that they lead to an inevitable conclusion. Every fact must be checked; related court decisions must be found and applied to the case at hand; objections must be dealt with. All this must be accomplished with the knowledge that those on the other side are doing the same thing.

The briefs serve as a primer on the case for the justices who must decide its outcome. Particularly eloquent arguments may sometimes find their way into the Court's opinion on the case.

THE *LOVING* BRIEF

Bernard Cohen and Philip Hirschkop, working with a team of ACLU lawyers and other legal experts, prepared the *Loving* brief. They used the jurisdictional statement and the arguments they had presented to the lower courts as a base. In addition, they consulted with psychologists and sociologists on the effects of interracial marriage on families and children, and researched the biological aspects.

THE CHILDREN OF RICHARD AND MILDRED LOVING PLAY IN 1965; FROM LEFT: PEGGY, DONALD, AND SIDNEY. THE LAWYERS FOR THE LOVINGS ARGUED THAT VIRGINIA'S LAWS PREVENTED CHILDREN OF INTERRACIAL COUPLES FROM RECEIVING BENEFITS AVAILABLE TO OFFSPRING OF PARENTS OF THE SAME RACE.

On February 17, 1967, the Lovings' lawyers submitted their forty-page brief to the Supreme Court. In it, they made six points:

· The entire ten sections of Virginia's antimiscegenation code should be abolished.

· Based on their history, Virginia's laws against interracial marriage were "relics of slavery and expressions of racism."

· Laws against interracial marriage caused "immeasurable social harm."

• Despite the historical record, the Fourteenth Amendment did not exempt state antimiscegenation laws from its requirements.

• Virginia's laws against interracial marriage were "racially discriminatory" and denied the Lovings "equal protection of the laws."

• The laws also violated the Fourteenth Amendment's due process clause.

The lawyers wasted no time stating their position in the brief and making clear their expectations of the Court. The case, they wrote, "gives this Court an appropriate opportunity to strike down the last remnants of legalized slavery in our country—the antimiscegenation laws of Virginia and sixteen other states." The United States, they noted, was the only "civilized country" in the world other than South Africa—that still banned interracial marriages.

After describing the case's journey through the legal system, the brief detailed the laws involved, including several Virginia statutes and the Fourteenth Amendment. It then proceeded to defend the Lovings' position.

ABOLISH THE CODE
It made no sense, the lawyers argued, to abolish only the two sections of the code levied against the Lovings. If that happened, the brief noted, the state could then punish the couple under other codes. Since their marriage would be void, the state could then charge them with living together without being married. Their children would lose the benefits available to offspring of legally married parents. In addition, the lawyers noted, the two sections of the code depended on another section (20-54) to define who, under Virginia law, was black and who was white. The

existing laws could also be used to punish interracial couples who were married legally elsewhere and who later moved into the state.

RELICS OF SLAVERY

The brief presented historical accounts that showed that Virginia's antimiscegenation laws arose from slave owners' concern that intermarriage would erode whites' power over blacks. Slavery reinforced the view that whites were superior to blacks. In addition, the accounts indicated early "religious prejudice" against Christians mixing with "heathens." Racial intolerance and antagonism toward blacks, the lawyers contended in the brief, led to the adoption of the Racial Integrity Act of 1924, which incorporated the old laws and added new ones to create Virginia's antimiscegenation codes. They argued that proponents of the act wanted to preserve the white race for the same reasons Hitler hoped to created a "super race." Virginia's form requiring couples about to be married to state their racial composition resembled tactics employed by Nazi Germany, according to the brief. In a footnote, the lawyers commented that if John Rolfe and Pocahontas had married in Virginia in 1966, they would have been guilty of violating Virginia's ban against whites marrying anyone with more than one-sixteenth of Indian blood.

IMMEASURABLE HARM

The lawyers then addressed "another history [that] lurks beneath the surface of the 'written' history. . . This is the story of what these laws have done to our entire people." The hidden story, according to the brief, revealed a pattern of rape by white masters on female slaves. The result of such atrocities was that as many as 83 percent of black Americans had a white ancestor, according to an expert cited in the brief.

The antimiscegenation laws, the lawyers noted, stood "as a present-day incarnation of an ancient evil." Such laws maintained the unequal status between black women and white men by barring marriage between them but making it relatively easy for white men to have sex with black partners. Marriage, but not illicit sex, gave the women status, according to the brief. "These laws do not simply bar interracial marriage, they perpetuate and foster illicit exploitative sex relationships."

The "ultimate evil" of such laws, the lawyers concluded, lay in the "open affront to the dignity" of black Americans, who were made to feel that they were "not good enough to marry a 'white person.'" The state's use of the antimiscegenation laws as an "official symbol of a caste system" reinforced the inferior status of blacks. It was up to the Court, as noted in the brief, to deal with such invidious laws.

NO EXEMPTION

Next, the lawyers examined the legislative history behind the Fourteenth Amendment in the brief. The debates used to bolster the state's case, according to the brief, revolved around the Civil Rights Act of 1866 and not the amendment itself. Furthermore, the debaters based their assumption that antimiscegenation laws would not be covered by the Fourteenth Amendment on discredited theories. If the Court believed that the amendment's protections should be limited, the lawyers argued, then it never could have issued the *Brown* ruling or ordered an end to segregation. Concluding their arguments in the brief, the lawyers maintained that the Court must rely on its own interpretation of the Fourteenth Amendment, not on "doubtful legislative history," when applying the amendment to the laws against interracial marriage.

DENIED EQUAL PROTECTION

The state of Virginia convicted Mildred and Richard Loving because of their race. If not for their race, the state would not have considered their marriage a crime, the brief said. Noting the Court's ruling to outlaw school segregation because it violated equal protection, the lawyers argued that the same reasoning should apply to the Lovings' case. The right to marry, they contended, was "even more fundamental than the right of students to attend an integrated public school."

The brief cited many cases in which the Court had struck down laws using race as a standard to treat people differently. When race was a factor, the brief noted, the Court required states to show an "overriding purpose" that made such classifications necessary.

One by one, the brief knocked down Virginia's reasons for justifying its antimiscegenation laws. Protecting "racial purity" was not a valid justification because, the brief noted, there was no evidence that a "pure" race existed. In addition, the laws did not protect the purity of all races, only that of the white race.

According to the brief, Virginia based its concept of "race" on "a combination of legal fiction and genetic nonsense . . . designed to preserve the social status of Virginia's politically dominant group." The argument that interracial marriage would "corrupt" the blood and "weaken" the white race could not be substantiated. All races, the brief said, were "essentially equal in native ability and capacity for civilization." Even if there were evidence that one race was inferior, the lawyers argued, it would not justify "the serious restriction on personal liberty" that a ban on interracial marriages would impose.

The brief also dismissed the argument that interracial marriages should be banned because they produced biologically inferior offspring. "There is not a single

UNESCO STATEMENT ON RACE AND INTERRACIAL MARRIAGE

Issued by the United Nations Educational Scientific and Cultural Organization, 1964

It has never been proved that interbreeding has biological disadvantages for mankind as a whole. On the contrary, it contributes to the maintenance of biological ties between human groups and thus to the unity of the species in its diversity.

The biological consequences of a marriage depend only on the individual genetic make-up of the couple and not on their race.

Therefore, no biological justification exists for prohibiting intermarriage between persons of different races, or for advising against it on racial grounds.

anthropologist teaching at a major university in the United States who subscribes to the theory that Negro-white matings cause biologically deleterious results," the brief noted.

A statement on race by world-renowned scientists, released by the United Nations Educational, Scientific and Cultural Organization (UNESCO), concurred.

The laws against interracial marriage, the brief stated, "deny Negroes and other nonwhites equal protection of the law and stamp them as inferior citizens." In a footnote at the end of the section, the lawyers quoted Judge Bazile's statement on the religious justification for antimiscegenation laws. The judge's words, the lawyers noted in the brief, "require[d] no comment."

VIOLATION OF DUE PROCESS

Finally, the brief argued, Virginia's antimiscegenation laws violated the Lovings' right to due process. "We think it clear that the 'liberty' which is protected by the due process clause of the Fourteenth Amendment includes the right to marry," the lawyers declared. While the state had the right to place some restrictions on marriage, the Constitution required that it have a "legitimate legislative purpose" for doing so. Virginia had no such legitimate reason for denying citizens the right to marry, the brief concluded.

The *Loving* lawyers ended with the assertion that the Court "should make clear that neither Virginia nor any other State can constitutionally prohibit or penalize interracial marriages." The antimiscegenation laws, they said, stood as the last legal remnants of segregation. "There are no laws more symbolic of the Negro's relegation to second-class citizenship," the brief proclaimed. "Whether or not this court has been wise to avoid this issue in the past, the time has come to strike down these laws; they are legalized racial prejudice, unsupported by reason or morals, and should not exist in a good society."

VIRGINIA STATES ITS CASE

Virginia Assistant Attorney General R. D. McIlwaine III had worked on several briefs for U.S. Supreme Court cases involving the state. An old hand at state politics, he now faced a particularly difficult challenge: to convince a Court that had already ruled that states could not segregate its public schools or discriminate based on race to let Virginia keep its race-based laws when it came to marriage.

The state's legal team—McIlwaine, Attorney General Robert Y. Button, and another assistant attorney general, Kenneth C. Patty—submitted their fifty-two-page brief on March 20, 1967. It began with a strong attack on the Lovings' contention that the Virginia code was unconstitutional. The matter had already been "thoroughly settled," the lawyers argued. In fact, there had been so many court rulings granting states the right to regulate their own affairs that the Court would have "to rewrite or amend the Fourteenth Amendment" to decide in the Lovings' favor.

Furthermore, the brief argued, it was not the Court's role to overturn state laws based on sociological, biological, and anthropological research. Quoting from the Virginia Supreme Court's decision in the *Naim* case, the brief said such actions by the Court would be "judicial legislation in the rawest sense of that term." The state, not the Court, used such evidence to determine which laws to pass. The Court, on the other hand, based its judgments on established legal doctrine.

Even if the Court reviewed the research, however, the material would provide no clear answer in the case, according to the brief. The justices would find themselves "mired in a Serbonian bog of conflicting scientific opinion upon the effects of interracial marriage."

The brief moved on to its main point: Virginia's anti-miscegenation codes did not violate the Fourteenth Amendment because the early leaders who wrote and enacted the amendment specifically exempted the codes from its provisions. Citing judicial codes and Court decisions, the brief asserted that in interpreting the Constitution, courts were required to follow the intent of the framers.

The lawyers devoted the next twenty-four pages to a review of the legislative history of the Fourteenth Amendment. The congressional debates leading up to the passage of the amendment, they argued, showed conclusively that the framers never intended to interfere with states' rights to regulate marriage. Although the statements supporting that argument occurred during debate on two previous bills—the Civil Rights Act of 1866 and the Freedmen's Bureau Bill—the brief argued that the comments revealed the intentions of Congress at the time when the Fourteenth Amendment was passed.

The brief quoted Illinois Senator Lyman Trumbull, among others. Trumbull reassured a fellow senator that the Civil Rights Act of 1866 would not interfere with Indiana's law prohibiting marriages between blacks and whites. "If the negro is denied the right to marry a white person, the white person is equally denied the right to marry the negro. I see no discrimination against either in this respect that does not apply to both," Trumbull is quoted as saying.

The next several pages of the brief cited decisions by both federal and state courts upholding the antimiscegenation laws. Beginning with the *Kinney* case and ending with Virginia Supreme Court's *Naim* decision, the rulings provided a "virtually uninterrupted line of judicial decisions . . . in which the constitutional validity of the State antimiscegenation statutes has been sustained," according to the brief.

The final argument centered on the scientific studies of interracial marriage. Such studies, the brief reiterated, had no relevance to the Court's review of the *Loving* case. Nevertheless, the next ten pages included a litany of researchers' objections to and reservations about interracial marriage.

The state's lawyers concluded the brief by relying on three U.S. Supreme Court decisions and borrowing once again from the Virginia Supreme Court ruling in *Naim*. An 1888 divorce and inheritance case, *Maynard* v. *Hill*, had stipulated that "marriage . . . has always been subject to the control of the Legislature." Likewise, a 1948 ruling in another divorce case, *Sherrer* v. *Sherrer*, had determined that "under the Constitution the regulation and control of marital and family relationships are reserved to the States." A third case, *Reynolds* v. *U.S.*, a bigamy case decided in 1878, noted that "government is necessarily required to deal" with the "social relations and social obligations and duties" of marriage. All four cases, they noted, bolstered their argument that the Constitution gave states the right to regulate marriage. The Virginia antimiscegenation codes, they declared, reflected a policy that had existed "for over two centuries [and that] have stood—compatibly with the Fourteenth Amendment . . . since that Amendment was adopted."

Amicus Curiae Briefs

Five additional briefs, submitted by *amicus curiae*, presented arguments in the case. Four supported the Lovings' claim and one, written by the state of North Carolina, argued for Virginia's position.

The Japanese American Citizens League, a national nonprofit group, was the only *amicus* granted permission to argue the case before the U.S. Supreme Court. The charitable organization dealt mainly with issues affecting Japanese Americans. The group petitioned to participate in the *Loving* case because of concern that antimiscegenation laws might be used to discriminate against Japanese Americans and because of the league's interest in the "dignity and liberty of all Americans." Only Georgia's law specifically included Japanese in its antimiscegenation code, but other states mentioned "Mongolians," members of the "Malay race," and "colored persons."

In its brief, the Japanese American Citizens League (JACL) focused on three points:

• The Court should overturn the decision in *Pace* v. *Alabama*. The 1883 ruling—that laws passed constitutional muster as long as they levied equal penalties on all offenders—relied on faulty reasoning and conflicted with more recent Supreme Court rulings. The brief argued that government laws based on race (even those with equal penalties) had "no proper place in controlling . . . the fundamental, basic and highly personal right of marriage." It added: "The freedom of choice,—the freedom of choice not to marry a person of another race as well as the freedom to marry another without regard to race,—should and must reside with the individual, not with the government."

• Virginia's antimiscegenation laws violated the equal protection rights of all Americans, white and nonwhite. The brief contended that the laws aimed to preserve the "purity" of the white race only; other races were of no concern. "An example of more unequal protection of the laws can hardly be summoned," the brief noted. The JACL lawyers added, however, that the solution was not to extend the policy of "racial purity" to all races. Such an action, the brief declared, would be the "antithesis to the establishment and maintenance of a democratic society of free men." The laws also robbed whites as well as nonwhites of the freedom to marry whom they chose, according to the brief. In addition, the vague terms and inconsistencies in the laws made it difficult to determine who could be arrested for what actions.

• Antimiscegenation laws were based on "fundamental misconceptions of fact" and served no "legitimate legislative purpose." The brief dismissed the racial theories on which Virginia had based its laws, arguing that they were false and presenting evidence to disprove them. The lawyers asserted that "racial purity" did not exist and therefore could not be preserved; that no race was superior to another; and that there was no biological evidence that interracial marriages were harmful.

The National Association for the Advancement of Colored People (NAACP) attacked the state's policy of preserving "racial integrity" in its brief. The organization, with chapters throughout the country, served as an advocate for black Americans. The NAACP had played a central role in the *Brown* decision as well as other suits urging the Court to outlaw segregation in public schools, transportation, and facilities. Its stated purpose was "to secure full and equal citizenship rights for [blacks] without restrictions, burdens, limitations or barriers based upon race or color."

In its brief the NAACP presented evidence, including the UNESCO statement, that discredited the notion of a "pure race," the theory that interracial marriages produced inferior offspring, and statements that tied culture to race. "Not only do the antimiscegenation statutes have no scientific basis, but their philosophy is an affront to millions of our citizens," the brief concluded.

The Legal Defense and Educational Fund of the NAACP filed its own *amicus* brief in the case. An outgrowth of the NAACP, the New York-based group formed to help black Americans file lawsuits to "secure their constitutional rights."

Its brief contended that the laws banning interracial marriage violated both the due process and the equal

A MAN JOINS THE NAACP DURING THE GROUP'S CAMPAIGN IN THE 1960S TO WIN EQUALITY FOR BLACK AMERICANS. LAWYERS FOR THE ORGANIZATION ARGUED IN THE *LOVING* CASE THAT LAWS AGAINST INTERRACIAL MARRIAGE PLACED NONWHITE CITIZENS IN AN INFERIOR POSITION TO WHITES.

protection clauses of the Fourteenth Amendment. The Court's previous rulings striking down racial segregation laws established that there could be "no justification for such laws and that they are all invalid." The brief repeated the NAACP arguments against Virginia's racial purity policy, citing much of the same evidence.

A coalition made up of Catholic bishops, the National Catholic Conference for Interracial Justice, and the National Catholic Social Action Committee filed a fourth *amicus* brief in favor of the Lovings. The bishops and the nonprofit groups became involved in the case because of their commitment "to end racial discrimination and prej udice" and because of the "serious issues of personal liberty" raised by the Lovings' ordeal.

The brief's arguments agreed with the issues raised by the other supporters of the Lovings. The brief also raised two additional points:

• The antimiscegenation laws interfered with Americans' right to religious freedom guaranteed in the First Amendment. Defining marriage as "a fundamental act of religion," the brief argued that states could impose limits on the religious act only by showing that it presented "a grave and immediate danger" to interests legally under the state's control. "Interracial marriages do not constitute a threat to the 'principles of government' made manifest in the United States Constitution," the brief asserted. It added, "The preservation of a racially segregated society is not an interest which the state may lawfully protect."

• The laws unconstitutionally denied Americans the right to have children. Because the laws prohibited marriages between blacks and whites, they also prevented people in those relationships from having children, according to the brief. "Such persons may have children only if they are willing to pay the penalty of having them legally denominated as bastards," according to the brief.

The lone *amicus* brief in support of the state came from the state of North Carolina, whose antimiscegenation laws resembled Virginia's. The state's six-page argument echoed the points made in the Virginia brief: The historical record of the Fourteenth Amendment's passage and previous court rulings supported the state's right to ban interracial marriages. The North Carolina lawyers also repeated Virginia's claim that interpretations of scientific research differed widely and that the legislature, not the Court, should be the one to consider such evidence.

With the briefs submitted, the Lovings' case now headed for the small but elegant courtroom where U.S. Supreme Court cases had been argued since 1935. What was said in that hushed room—and how the justices interpreted those words—might well determine the fate of interracial couples for generations to come.

SIX
BEFORE THE COURT

For more than two centuries, U.S. Supreme Court sessions have opened with the same pronouncement: "The Honorable, the Chief Justice and the Associate Justices of the Supreme Court of the United States. Oyez! Oyez! Oyez! All persons having business before the Honorable, the Supreme Court of the United States, are admonished to draw near and give their attention, for the Court is now sitting. God save the United States and this Honorable Court!"

Court sessions begin at 10 a.m. sharp, Monday through Wednesday. Those in the formal courtroom rise as the nine black-robed justices file from the opening between the red velvet curtains that hide the inner chambers from view. The chief justice takes his seat at the raised bench first. Following tradition, the associate justices take their assigned seats, with the longest-serving associate justice sitting at the right of the chief justice; the associate justice next in seniority takes a seat to the chief justice's left and so on down the line.

After the justices are seated, they deal with any business before the Court. On Monday mornings, the Court releases a list of cases the justices have accepted or rejected for review. Opinions are usually read on Tuesday

one SIZE DIDN'T FIT ALL

A visitor to the Supreme Court in the 1960s may have wondered why the justices' chairs did not match. Some were short; others had high backs. All were cushioned and covered in black leather, but some were tufted, some smooth. In a way, the chairs reflected the uniqueness of the justices who sat in them. When the Court moved to its own building in 1935, leather bench chairs were provided for the justices. Some of the justices, however, brought their own chairs, creating a jumble of styles and shapes. In 1969 Chief Justice Warren Burger requested that his chair be modeled after the high-backed bench chair used at the time by Justice Byron White. After that, bench chairs of the same model were fashioned for each incoming justice. Today the chairs have a uniform look and style, although they are adjusted to fit each individual justice. As part of the Court's tradition, when a justice retires, the other justices buy his or her chair and present it as a going-away gift. Then a new chair—designed especially for the new justice—takes its place behind the bench.

and Wednesday mornings and on the third Monday of the months when the Court is in session. The chief justice calls for a recess for lunch from noon until 1 p.m. Public sessions end at 3 p.m.

Justices work year-round, studying briefs, considering requests for review, researching and writing opinions, discussing cases, and performing other duties.

Public sessions are held from October through late June or early July, and justices hear oral arguments from October through April. For these seven months, the Court alternates between two weeks or so of open sessions, or sittings, during which the justices hear oral arguments and read opinions, and two weeks during which the Court is in recess. Recesses provide time for the justices to review oral arguments, discuss cases and decide their outcome, and write decisions.

Lawyers arguing before the U.S. Supreme Court follow a strict code of conduct. A twenty-one page guidebook prepared by the clerk of the Court offers lawyers appearing before the Court for the first time tips on how to address the justices, where to sit, when and how long to speak, and even what to wear. Lawyers are expected to wear "dark conservative business dress (e.g., navy blue or charcoal gray)."

FOR THE APPELLANTS, PART I

On April 10, 1967, the lawyers walked up the marble steps to the U.S. Supreme Court building to present their arguments. The two ACLU lawyers, Philip Hirschkop and Bernard Cohen, argued the case for the Lovings. They split the time, with Hirschkop addressing the equal protection argument first, followed by Cohen, who focused on due process. Hirschkop had earned his law degree only two years before and was just thirty years old when he faced the nation's highest court. To qualify to argue before the U.S. Supreme Court, a lawyer had to have been admitted to the highest court in a state or territory (or the District of Columbia) for at least three years. Since Hirschkop did not meet that requirement, the Court granted the young lawyer special leave (known as *pro hac vice* or "for this occasion") to argue the case.

The wives of the two attorneys and other members of

the legal team sat in the courtroom waiting for the arguments to begin. The Lovings—whose marriage had sparked this monumental debate—did not attend.

Led by Chief Justice Earl Warren, the nine members of the Court walked into the room and settled into their chairs. In addition to the chief justice, associate justices Hugo L. Black, William O. Douglas, Tom C. Clark, John Marshall Harlan, William J. Brennan Jr., Potter Stewart, Byron White, and Abe Fortas would hear the arguments in the *Loving* case.

Chief Justice Warren commanded attention as he read out the name of the case. After granting Cohen's motion that the Court grant his co-counsel permission to argue the case, Warren signaled Hirschkop to begin. Despite his youth and inexperience, Hirschkop began with a confident attack on Virginia's antimiscegenation laws, referring to them as "the most odious of the segregation laws and the slavery laws." Novelist Norman Mailer, who later hired Hirschkop to defend him against disorderly conduct charges during a 1967 antiwar march on the Pentagon, once compared the lawyer to a "wildly successful salesman with an impossibly difficult buyer."

In his New York accent, the young lawyer urged the Court to consider the entire Virginia code on intermarriage when making its ruling, not just the two sections, 20-58 and 20-59, under which the Lovings had been charged. Section 20-58 made it illegal to leave the state to get married to someone of a different race with the intention of returning to live as husband and wife. Section 20-59 set the punishment for marriage between a white person and a "colored" person at one to five years in the state penitentiary. Intermarriage, according to Virginia law, was a felony.

Hirschkop noted that other sections of the Virginia code voided marriages between blacks and whites. If the

Court ruled only that Sections 20-58 and 20-59 were invalid, the state could arrest the Lovings for living together without being married (against the law in Virginia and several other states at the time). Under the state code, the Loving children would be considered illegitimate and would not be eligible to collect insurance and Social Security benefits if their parents died.

To prevent the state from further harassing the Lovings, Hirschkop asked the Court to rule on the whole question of interracial marriage. "We strongly urge the Court when considering this to consider this basic question: May a state proscribe a marriage between such individuals because of their race and their race alone?"

In answer to a justice's question, Hirschkop said that sixteen states had laws banning interracial marriage. All were in the South or bordered southern states. One state, Maryland, had recently repealed such a law, and two others, Missouri and Oklahoma, had introduced bills but had failed in an attempt to repeal their laws.

With that, the Lovings' lawyer launched into the heart of his argument: that laws banning interracial marriage violated the Constitution's guarantee of equal protection. "They violate the Fourteenth Amendment," Hirschkop told the justices. He disputed Virginia's contention that marriage fell under health and welfare laws, which the state had a right to legislate for itself. "We hope to show the Court that these are not health and welfare laws," he said. "These are slavery laws pure and simple."

Then, with few interruptions from the justices, Hirschkop outlined the history of laws banning interracial marriage dating back to the 1600s. Those early laws, he noted, focused on unions between white men and black women and whether their offspring would be slaves or free. "It was a slavery law," the lawyer told the Court, "and it was only concerned with one thing . . . the purity of the white woman, not the purity of the Negro woman." Such laws, he said, "rob the Negro race of their dignity" and "hold the Negro class in a lower position."

For the next two centuries, Hirschkop said, southerners and others tried to define "who these people were that they were proscribing." In 1705, he said, a Negro (the term used at the time for Americans with African ancestry) was defined as a person with one-eighth of Negro blood. Later that century, in 1785, the definition shifted to people with one-quarter of Negro ancestry. Virginia finally adopted a legal definition of a Negro in 1930 as "a person of any traceable Negro blood." Hirschkop commented that such a definition "defies any scientific interpretation."

The lawyer quoted the 1878 case of *Kinney* v. *Commonwealth* to demonstrate Virginia's public policy of preventing "spurious issue"—the offspring of mixed races—and of protecting "cherished southern civilization." But, Hirschkop told the Court, "they didn't speak about the southern civilization as a whole, but this white civilization. And they want the races kept distinct and separate. . . . They talk about alliances so unnatural that God has forbidden them." The state's position, the lawyer noted, echoed the arguments rejected by the Court in the *Brown* case.

Race HYSTeria

He continued with a discussion of the hysteria over race that swept the United States in the 1920s. In the American West, he noted, whites who believed that Chinese and Japanese immigrants threatened their existence warned of the "Yellow Peril." Northerners feared the influx of Italian and Irish immigrants. Such anxieties fueled talk of race suicide, bolstered support for eugenics, and led to the push to pass antimiscegenation laws, Hirschkop told the Court. "That's when the Virginia Legislature passed our current

AN INFLUX OF WORKERS AND THEIR FAMILIES FROM CHINA LED SOME WESTERNERS TO WARN OF A "YELLOW PERIL" THAT WOULD THREATEN THE WHITE CITIZENRY. HERE, A MAN AND HIS CHILDREN WALK NEAR THE CHINESE CONSULATE IN SAN FRANCISCO.

body of law. They took all these old laws, these antebellum and postbellum laws, and they put them together into what we presently have," he said.

Answering a question posed by Chief Justice Warren, Hirschkop noted that many states, including those in the West and the North, already had laws that banned interracial marriage. But Virginia's 1924 antimiscegenation laws were considered to be model legislation. Only Georgia, however, adopted Virginia's code. After the 1954 *Brown* v. *Board of Education* decision, Hirschkop said, thirteen states repealed their antimiscegenation laws.

Virginia's law, entitled "A Bill to Preserve the Integrity of the White Race," was passed in 1924 to preserve racial integrity of the white race only, Hirschkop told the Court. Although the state's laws required that white people marry only other whites, the laws made intermarriage a crime only when it involved blacks and whites. Asians could marry blacks, the lawyer noted. State law voided marriages between Asians and whites, but such an intermarriage did not carry a criminal penalty for the Asian. Virginia lawmakers, Hirschkop said, "were not concerned with racial integrity but racial supremacy of the white race. . . . These laws, your honors, are ludicrous in their inception and equally ludicrous in their application."

The lawyer then looked at similar laws in other southern states. Under North Carolina law, he noted, Cherokee Indians living in one county were considered whites; those living in other counties fell into the Negro category. In Mississippi, he said, advocates of intermarriage could face up to five years in jail under the criminal code. He called ridiculous a Georgia court decision that suggested offspring of mixed marriages were effeminate.

Referring to Virginia's brief in the case, Hirschkop quoted from another Virginia Supreme Court decision cited by the state, *Naim* v. *Naim*. In that case, the lawyer noted, the state "wanted to preserve the racial integrity of their citizens. They want not to have a 'mongrel breed of citizens.'" The court ruled in the *Naim* case that the Constitution did not bar states from passing laws "to prevent the obliteration of racial pride"; neither did the Constitution require that the state "must permit the corruption of blood even though it weaken and destroy the quality of the citizenship."

Hirschkop also quoted Judge Leon Bazile's ruling against the Lovings: "Almighty God created the races, white, black, Malay, yellow, red, and placed them on separate continents." Calling the statement "fundamentally ludicrous," the lawyer dismissed all such sentiments and the laws based on them.

"We feel the very basic wrong of these statutes is they rob the Negro race of their dignity," he told the Court. "And fundamental in the concept of liberty in the Fourteenth Amendment is the dignity of the individual, because without that there is no ordered liberty."

HISTOry OF DeBaTeS

The lawyer disputed his opponent's argument that the post-Civil War Congress had never intended for the Fourteenth Amendment to interfere with antimiscegenation laws. The state of Virginia used the 1866 debates leading up to the passage of the Civil Rights Act of 1866 and the Freedmen's Bureau Bill to make its point. But Hirschkop pointed out that the debates cited were not about the Fourteenth Amendment. The guarantees provided by the Fourteenth Amendment, the lawyer contended, were "much broader in scope" than those included in the earlier bills. And, he argued, the debates did not give a clear picture of what Congress intended regarding intermarriage. "It's up to the Court to decide what happened," he told the justices.

U.S. REPUBLICAN SENATOR LYMAN TRUMBULL SPONSORED THE CIVIL RIGHTS ACT OF 1866 IN THE SENATE. HE ALSO SUPPORTED PRESIDENT ANDREW JOHNSON DURING HIS IMPEACHMENT TRIAL.

Even so, Hirschkop said, the debates themselves—and in particular the comments of Senator Lyman Trumbull—discounted the state's theory. The lawyer noted that Trumbull had said the bills under consideration would not

repeal the antimiscegenation laws "if there is no discrimination [in the laws]." Hirschkop argued that Virginia's
laws on intermarriage were "clearly discriminatory."

Those coming before the Court had frequently tried
to argue that the Fourteenth Amendment did not apply to
their particular case, Hirschkop said. But in *McLaughlin*
v. *Florida*, the case of an unmarried interracial couple
convicted of illegally living together, the Court had ruled
that the Fourteenth Amendment's central purpose was to
eliminate racial discrimination in the states. Hirschkop
strongly supported that statement, arguing that it should
also apply to the *Loving* case. Virginia's laws against interracial marriage, he reiterated, were "slavery laws" and
were enacted "to keep the slaves in their place." And, he
added, "the Virginia laws still view the Negro race as a
slave race."

Hirschkop concluded his part of the argument with a
strong plea that the justices throw out the entire Virginia
code on interracial marriage. "These are the most odious
laws to come before the Court," he said. "They rob the
Negro race of its dignity. And only a decision that will reach
the full body of these laws of the state of Virginia will
change that."

FOR THE APPELLANTS, PART II

Bernard Cohen took his place before the nine justices.
Charged with the task of presenting the due process argument, he faced tougher questioning from the justices. He
began by citing several cases to support his point of view.
The Court had already ruled in *Meyer* v. *Nebraska* and
Skinner v. *Oklahoma* that marriage was "a fundamental
right or liberty," Cohen noted.

Justice Stewart asked whether Cohen would agree that
states had the right to forbid brothers and sisters from
marrying each other.

Cohen conceded that such limits were proper, as was the Court's ban on polygamy, or marriage to more than one person. But, he added, such limits did not involve race.

The justice, however, questioned Cohen's intent. "You're not arguing the race question; you're arguing complete freedom to contract, aren't you, under the due process clause?"

Cohen noted that the Court could—and should—rule in the Lovings' favor based on the Fourteenth Amendment's guarantee of equal protection that barred racial discrimination. However, he did not abandon his due process argument. The state had a right to regulate marriage, including a ban on marriage between first cousins, but, he said, such restrictions had to be based on reasonable grounds. In this case, he argued, "the state cannot infringe upon the right of Richard and Mildred Loving to marry because of race. These are just not acceptable grounds."

A justice asked whether any efforts had been made to repeal the antimiscegenation laws in Virginia. Candidates making such an attempt would face "political suicide," Cohen replied.

Justice Black steered the discussion back to the due process argument. If the Court ruled on the equal protection argument, he asked, why even consider due process?

In reply, Cohen urged the Court's support for both arguments. Like Hirschkop, he expressed concern that a too-narrow decision might provide a loophole that would allow the state to continue its ban against interracial marriages. In addition to the criminal sanctions applied against the Lovings, other sections in the Virginia antimiscegenation laws should be abolished, Cohen argued. He cited the state's requirement that a couple obtain a racial composition certificate indicating each person's race before marrying. According to Cohen, the clerk could decide who was black and who was white. Acknowledging that certificates had not been used in recent years, Cohen said the law could nevertheless be applied to prevent people from marrying based on race.

The next question must have cheered Cohen and the *Loving* advocates. Could these laws still apply, the justice asked, "if the Court should decide straight out that the state cannot prevent marriage . . . between the whites and the blacks because of their color?" Wouldn't that ruling, he went on, settle the matter constitutionally?

Cohen quickly agreed. And he noted that no matter which argument was made, the issue remained one of fundamental fairness. He quoted Richard Loving's words, among the most memorable of the case: "'Tell the Court, I love my wife," Loving had said to Cohen, "and it is just unfair that I can't live with her in Virginia."

Next, Cohen addressed the state's contention that the enactors of the Fourteenth Amendment had never intended to ban antimiscegenation laws. He argued that only a handful of senators even mentioned such laws, and those comments were made during debate on the Freedmen's Bureau Bill or the Civil Rights Act of 1866. "Nowhere has the state been able to cite one item of legislative debate on the Fourteenth Amendment itself with respect to antimiscegenation statutes," Cohen told the Court. Further, he noted, the state's own brief showed that just as many senators believed the Civil Rights Act of 1866 would abolish laws against interracial marriage. "At best, the legislative history is inconclusive," he said.

In other cases, Cohen pointed out, the Court had ruled that the Fourteenth Amendment was not limited to situations and attitudes existing when it became law. "As this Court has found before . . . the Fourteenth Amendment is an amendment which grows and can be applied to situations as our knowledge becomes greater and as our progress is made," he said. Therefore, he argued, the Court should have no problem in finding that Virginia's codes on interracial marriage were "odious to the Fourteenth Amendment."

Cohen concluded his argument with questions of his own: "What is the danger to the state of Virginia of interracial marriage? What is the state of the danger to the people of interracial marriage?" He would use the final minutes allotted to him to rebut the state's arguments.

SUPPORT FOR THE LOVINGS

Occasionally the U.S. Supreme Court allows someone other than the appellee and the appellant to participate in oral arguments. In the *Loving* case, the Court had invited the Japanese American Citizens' League, one of the organizations filing an *amicus* brief supporting the Lovings, to speak on the matter. Now Chief Justice Warren asked William Marutani, the league's attorney, to present his arguments. He would have fifteen minutes to make his case.

Marutani began with a personal comment about race. As the offspring of two parents from Japan, he noted that he was probably one of the few in the courtroom who could "declare with some degree of certainty" his race. Those of "white" ancestry, he said, would be hard-pressed to prove they had "no trace whatever of any blood other than Caucasian" as required under Virginia law, given the number of invasions, migrations, and "inevitable crossbreeding" in Europe and the "melting pot of America."

Although most anthropologists flatly rejected the notion of a "pure" race, Marutani said, the state of Virginia gave clerks and deputy clerks the power to judge whether marriage applicants were of a "pure white race." Judges and juries in Virginia could levy fines and punishments against people based on a term—pure white race— that did not even have a scientific definition. "This is vagueness in its grossest sense," he told the justices. The lawyer quoted a previous decision, *Giaccio v. Pennsylvania*, in which the Court had ruled that a law "which leaves judges and juries free to decide without any legally fixed standards what is prohibited and what is not in each particular case fails to meet the requirements of the due process clause."

Even if Virginia used an accepted standard when judging people's race, however, the laws against interracial marriage would still be unconstitutional, Marutani told the Court. These laws—aimed at preserving physical characteristics such as the size of the nose or the texture of the hair—"serve no proper legislative purpose," according to Marutani. He described the goal of preserving "meaningless and neutral" physical differences as "utter absurdity." Such laws, he argued, took marriage, "otherwise blessed by the state," and transformed it into a crime, based solely on race.

He, too, cited the *McLaughlin* decision, in which the Court ruled against a state law because it was based on race and "thus laid an unequal hand on those who committed . . . the same quality of offense." Under Virginia law, Marutani noted, Richard and Mildred Loving committed a crime not because of their marriage, but because of their race. "It was their race which made it an offense," he told the justices. And, the lawyer added, even though Richard Loving admitted he was white, he could not say for certain that he had "no trace whatever of any blood other than Caucasian."

Furthermore, Virginia applied the laws against interracial marriage unequally, the lawyer argued. He quoted the state's reasons for its ban on marriages between people of different races: to maintain "purity of public morals, preservation of racial integrity, as well as racial pride and to prevent a mongrel breed of citizens." But,

Marutani noted, Virginia laws barred only marriages between white people and partners of other races. Nonwhites were free to marry outside their race. "Virginia's laws are exposed for exactly what they are: a concept based upon racial superiority, that of the white race and white race only," Marutani said.

By striking down the laws against interracial marriage, the lawyer said, the Court would not force people to violate their beliefs. People would not be required to marry outside their race, only to have the freedom to marry the partner of their choice.

Would the law be good, Chief Justice Warren wanted to know, if no one was allowed to marry someone of another race?

No, replied Marutani. "First of all," he told the chief justice, "it is no answer to compound what we believe to be wrong." In addition, he said, not even experts agreed on how many races there were or how to identify them. The reason he had raised the issue—that the law was applied only to marriages with whites—was not to push for a ban on all interracial marriages but "to expose this law for exactly what it is . . . a white supremacy law," he said.

Justice Black followed with another question: Did Japan have laws that banned marriages between Japanese and whites? Marutani, born and raised in the United States, replied that he did not know. But, he said, custom dictated that Japanese, including his own mother, strongly opposed marriages with other races.

In another exchange, the lawyer—perhaps betraying his nervousness—referred to Justice Stewart as "Justice Potter." The Court did not correct him. Like Cohen, Marutani conceded that states could set standards for marriage—age, number of spouses, and other requirements. But he noted that those requirements applied "to all races without any distinction." He said Virginia's racial

JUSTICE HUGO BLACK ASKED ABOUT INTERRACIAL MARRIAGE BANS IN JAPAN.

requirements could not be considered in the same category as other standards applied to marriage because "they are superimposed over and above all these other standards."

FOR THE STATE

At the chief justice's invitation, Virginia Assistant Attorney General R. D. McIlwaine III rose to present the state's case. For him, the Supreme Court was familiar turf. As one of the state's top litigators, McIlwaine had been a central figure in several U.S. Supreme Court cases that pitted Virginia against aggrieved citizens. In 1963 he appeared before the Court in support of Virginia's voting districts, which favored certain groups over others. A year later, McIlwaine returned to the Supreme Court on behalf of the state in a case that attempted to circumvent the *Brown* v. *Board of Education* ruling requiring school desegregation. Before the Court once again in 1966, the state's lawyer argued—in an attempt to invalidate the Voting Rights Act of 1965—that the Constitution barred the federal government from interfering with state election laws. In all three cases, McIlwaine argued for the state's right to determine its own policies, regardless of federal laws and court rulings to the contrary. And in all three cases the Supreme Court ruled against him.

As he began his arguments in the *Loving* case, he faced similar skepticism from the same justices who had disposed of his previous arguments. Chief Justice Warren, in particular, posed sharp questions to the state official.

McIlwaine began by emphasizing that the case involved only two sections, 20-58 and 20-59, of the Virginia code. He argued strenuously that the Court should consider only those two sections. The justices, he said, could not properly rule on other Virginia laws, including the provision requiring certificates of racial composition. The justices, however, had no intention of ignoring the rest of Virginia's antimiscegenation codes. Chief Justice Warren asked the first of many questions on the matter. He noted that one state law allowed people with one-sixteenth or less of Indian blood to marry white people, while the law in the *Loving* case denied people with "a drop of colored blood in them" from marrying whites. Did that not raise questions of equal protection under the law? Warren asked.

While admitting that the law, section 20-54, might raise constitutional objections, McIlwaine reiterated his argument that the law was not before the Court for consideration. Responding to another question by Warren, the assistant attorney general said that whites and blacks made up 99.44 percent of Virginia's population. The state had so few people of other races, he said, that interracial marriage among them was "not a problem" and did not require a statute forbidding the practice.

Justice Harlan shifted the questioning to focus on Virginia's treatment of out-of-state couples. Did state law forbid an interracial couple from New York from moving into Virginia? he asked.

It did not, McIlwaine replied. But, he added, the couple's marriage might be void under Virginia law if it involved a white person and a black person. He noted that might conflict with federal law "that a marriage valid where celebrated is valid everywhere." But, he said, it was "highly questionable" that Virginia would recognize such a marriage because it would be contrary to "the strong local public policy" against such a union.

A LOOK AT HISTORY
McIlwaine quickly moved on to a discussion of his two main arguments for retaining the state laws on interracial marriage. The first focused on the Fourteenth Amendment and the history of its passage. The debates leading to

JUSTICE JOHN MARSHALL HARLAN

its passage, he said, showed that the amendment was never intended to infringe the power of the state to ban interracial marriage. Such laws were already in place at the time, he noted, and the leaders considering the amendment "specifically excluded" the Court from overriding the laws.

In arguing his second point, McIlwaine contended that even if the Court ruled that the Fourteenth Amendment did apply to interracial marriage laws, Virginia's laws served "a legitimate legislative objective of preventing the sociological and psychological evils which attend interracial marriages." The state, he added, had a right to adopt the laws, which he described as "a rational expression" of public policy.

Under questioning from Chief Justice Warren, McIlwaine was forced to admit that the debates to which he referred were not over the Fourteenth Amendment, but about the Freedmen's Bureau Bill and the Civil Rights Act of 1866. But the lawyer noted that the Civil Rights Act essentially became the first section of the Fourteenth Amendment. The discussion of states' rights, he said, had been "so completely settled" in the debates on the two bills that leaders saw no need to reopen the discussion when considering the amendment.

"No one who voted for, sponsored, or espoused the Civil Rights Act of 1866 dared to suggest that it would have the effect of invalidating state antimiscegenation statutes," McIlwaine argued. Congressional leaders had the same attitude toward interracial marriage laws when they adopted the Fourteenth Amendment, the lawyer contended.

Far from settling the matter, the lawyer's interpretation of history raised more questions. One justice noted that the *McLaughlin* decision—which struck down Florida's law barring black and white couples from living together—

supported the Lovings' position. In addition, the *McLaughlin* decision overturned a previous Court ruling (*Pace* v. *Alabama*), which had allowed a similar law to stand because the penalty was the same for both black and white partners. In repudiating the previous ruling, the Court said the decision was too narrow. Even with equal penalties, the law discriminated against blacks, according to the *McLaughlin* ruling. One justice suggested that if the Court had accepted McIlwaine's view of the Fourteenth Amendment's legislative history, perhaps the decision in the *McLaughlin* case would have been different.

McIlwaine countered that the *McLaughlin* ruling did not depend upon legislative history. In fact, he noted, the Court had intentionally set aside any review of the Fourteenth Amendment's history in deciding the *McLaughlin* case. Virginia had not relied on the *Pace* ruling, he said.

The state's lawyer turned instead to the *Brown* v. *Board of Education* case. He noted that the Court had ordered lawyers in that case to review the legislative history of the Fourteenth Amendment to determine whether Congress had foreseen that the amendment would abolish segregation in schools. The Court concluded that the history on the matter was unclear. But in the case of interracial marriage, McIlwaine argued, "the legislative history . . . is all one way"—the framers did not believe that the amendment would prevent states from barring interracial marriage.

A justice challenged McIlwaine further, asking if the lawyer was claiming that even if the framers were wrong, "even if they intended to exclude [interracial marriage] for the wrong reason, they nevertheless intended to exclude it?" (The justices are not identified by name in the transcripts or on the oral recordings.)

McIlwaine agreed that was correct, adding that a present-day Court's interpretation could not change the intent of framers "dead and buried." He noted that Congress intended for the amendment to have no effect on the state's power over marriage as long as the laws did not discriminate against anyone. If a state's law had set different penalties for black and white partners in an interracial marriage, then the framers would have found the law to be unconstitutional, McIlwaine said. But, he noted, Virginia's laws provided the same penalty for both partners.

A justice again noted, however, that Congress had not been debating the Fourteenth Amendment when such comments had been made.

McIlwaine agreed but repeated his claim that the discussions had occurred during the time when Congress was considering the amendment. "If the legislative history is given effect in this case," McIlwaine told the Court, "the statute of Virginia cannot be held to violate it."

After a short recess, McIlwaine resumed his argument. He summed up his discussion of legislative history by quoting Justice Black's words in a previous case:

> I see no reason to read into the Constitution meanings it did not have when it was adopted and which have not been put into it since. The proceedings of the original Constitutional Convention show beyond all doubt the power to veto a state's laws was denied Congress.

Again, a justice challenged McIlwaine on his assertion that the Fourteenth Amendment did not apply to Virginia's marriage laws. The legislative history aside, he said, wasn't it clear that the amendment's equal protection clause was enacted to ensure that states had to treat blacks and whites equally under the law? "Isn't that what the equal protection clause means?"

Once again McIlwaine agreed with the justice. Not willing to concede his point, though, he repeated his argument. The framers clearly understood that the interracial marriage law, with the same penalty for both parties, "did treat the individuals of both races equally."

JUSTIFYING THE LAWS

The lawyer then tackled his second point, that Virginia's laws against interracial marriage were reasonable and justifiable, and as such, did not violate the Constitution. "The prevailing climate of scientific opinion," he said, supported a ban on interracial marriage. Those who married outside their race, according to McIlwaine, had to endure greater pressures than those who married people of the same race. This caused unstable marriages, which harmed society as a whole.

Chief Justice Warren interjected with a comment that some people felt the same way about marriages between those of different religious faiths. Warren, a Protestant, had a daughter who was married to a Jewish man. "Do you think this state could prohibit people from having interreligious marriages," the chief justice asked.

McIlwaine replied that the evidence against interracial marriages was stronger than that against marriages involving different religions. He based his argument on a book by Dr. Albert I. Gordon, a rabbi who had studied the psychosocial effects of marriages between couples of different races, faiths, and cultures. The lawyer cited Gordon's conclusions that couples with such differences had more divorces and annulments than those who married people of the same race and background.

Perhaps the reason such couples had difficulty, suggested a justice, was because of laws like Virginia's and "the attitudes that those laws reflect."

McIlwaine agreed that society's attitudes caused

problems for couples of different backgrounds and their children. He noted that Gordon found no reason to prevent such marriages based on biology or genetics, but the author argued against them because of the psychological damage caused to the couples and their children.

Chief Justice Warren asked McIlwaine's opinion of UNESCO's statement on race, which had dismissed arguments against interracial marriage. Warren noted that the statement had been developed by "about twenty of the greatest anthropologists in the world," who had made "some very cogent findings on the races."

McIlwaine pointed out that the UNESCO experts had not produced conclusive evidence that intermarriage produced no harmful effects. Instead, he noted, the statement took the position that there was "no reliable evidence" of harmful consequences. Secondly, he said, not all scientists agreed with the UNESCO conclusions.

And not all scientists agreed with Gordon, McIlwaine's expert, did they? countered Chief Justice Warren.

McIlwaine agreed, but added that no one had disputed the statistics reported in Gordon's work.

Chief Justice Warren turned his attention back to the UNESCO statement, quoting the last paragraph:

> The biological data given above stand in open contradiction to the tenets of racism. Racist theories can in no way pretend to have any scientific foundation, and the anthropologists should endeavor to prevent the results of their researches from being used in such a biased way that they would serve nonscientific ends.

"It's a definite finding, it seems to me," he told McIlwaine.

In answer, the state's attorney detailed criticism of the

UNESCO statement by other experts. But he agreed with Warren that the Court could not settle the controversy. "The court would find itself mired in a Serbonian bog of conflicting scientific opinions which . . . is sufficiently broad, sufficiently fluid, and sufficiently deep to swallow up the entire federal judiciary," McIlwaine said, repeating the phrase he had used in his brief.

Justice Black turned to the Virginia code itself and the reasons behind its adoption. "Is there any doubt in your mind," he asked McIlwaine, "that the object of these statutes, the basic principle upon which they rest, is that the white people are superior to the colored people and should not be permitted to marry them?"

McIlwaine at first tried to separate the two sections of the law in the *Loving* case from section 20-54, which he admitted had been formed on that basis. But under continued questioning, the lawyer acknowledged that the state legislature had passed the code based on a belief that white people were superior. Nevertheless, he argued, the prohibition against intermarriage applied to people of both races.

Even with the same prohibition, Justice Black noted, it was "common sense . . . that [the ban was] the result of the old slavery days and the old feeling that the white man is superior to the colored man, which was exactly what the Fourteenth Amendment was adopted to prevent."

McIlwaine defended his position, repeating his previous arguments, but the justices continued to press the point. The law might keep the white race "pure," Chief Justice Warren said, but did it protect other races? "You don't have any prohibition against a Negro marrying a Malay or a Mongolian," he noted.

The lawyer reiterated that the state had few residents' of other races. The legislature, he argued, was not required to deal with "any social evil . . . resulting from

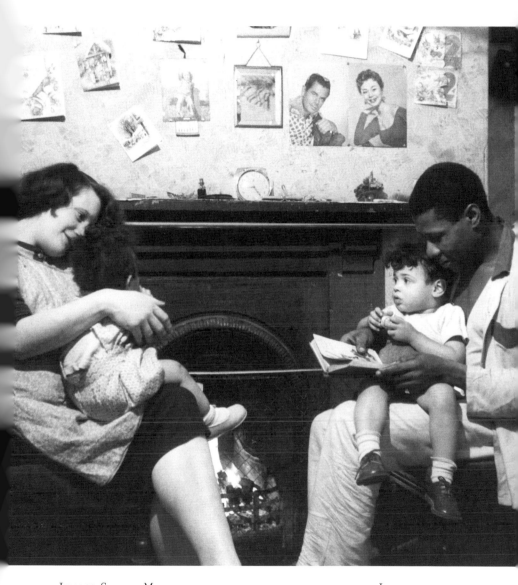

IN 1955, SIEBERT MATTISON, A BLACK FOUNDRY WORKER WHO LEFT JAMAICA IN 1947, SITS WITH HIS WELSH WIFE AND THEIR CHILDREN IN THEIR ONE-ROOM HOME IN BIRMINGHAM, ALABAMA. DESPITE THE SUPREME COURT'S DECISION IN THE *LOVING* CASE, ALABAMA RETAINED A BAN ON MARRIAGES BETWEEN BLACKS AND WHITES UNTIL 2000.

interracial marriage between Negroes and Malays or whites and Malays because there [was] no significant population distribution to that extent in Virginia."

The explanation did not satisfy Warren. "You mean on principle because there are only a few people of one race in Virginia that Virginia can say they have no rights?" he asked. "You're saying they don't have the same rights as the other race, the white race, to keep their race pure."

McIlwaine's explanation that the small number of people of other races posed no problem to the state failed to satisfy the Court. That comment elicited a disgusted "Well!—" from the chief justice.

Trying to regain lost ground, the lawyer quoted an expert on antimiscegenation laws: "Coverage of other races in the South is hardly necessary since they scarcely exist."

The justices, however, persisted. They quizzed McIlwaine on the state's definition of "colored," on the codes not directly leveled against the Lovings, and on the charges an out-of-state interracial married couple would face in Virginia (criminal misdemeanor charges for illicit cohabitation).

presenTInG THe EVIDence
McIlwaine devoted much of the remainder of his time quoting sources supporting his argument. In the face of evidence that interracial marriage had adverse effects on couples, children, and society as a whole, he argued, the state had the authority to ban such marriages. He noted that for more than a century since the adoption of the Fourteenth Amendment, states had regulated interracial marriage. Until the *Loving* case, sixteen continued to do so "without any question being raised as to the authority of the states to exercise this power."

The lawyer's mention of the sixteen states led to another exchange with the chief justice. Warren noted that all sixteen had been among those states with segregated schools. Although the chief justice said that the revelation was not "a matter of any great consequence," it did serve to link the interracial marriage codes with the segregation laws that the Court had taken a strong stand against. An ominous sign, perhaps, for Virginia's side in the case under discussion.

McIlwaine noted that, in 1950, thirty states, including several in the West, had antimiscegenation laws. All but the sixteen states mentioned earlier had repealed them. That showed, according to McIlwaine, that individual state legislatures should—and could—deal with the issue themselves.

Before sitting down, McIlwaine tackled one more concern raised by the justices: How could he justify the state's interracial marriage ban in light of the Court's decision in *Brown* v. *Board of Education*? The lawyer tried to differentiate the right to education and the right to marry. "There is no requirement that people marry and therefore a statute which forbids marriage is not the same as forbidding children to receive education," he told the justices.

For the Court to rule against the Virginia code, he argued, the justices would have to ignore "the interest of the state" and "the valid scientific evidence that exists on the detrimental effects of interracial marriage." Even rights, he noted, were "subject to reasonable limitations by the state." And banning interracial marriage, he contended, was as reasonable as prohibiting incestuous or polygamous marriages.

Again, the chief justice challenged McIlwaine's argument. "Didn't the segregation cases also argue to us what was supposed to be scientific evidence to the effect that the whites would be injured by having to go to school with the Negroes?" Warren asked the lawyer.

With his time at an end, McIlwaine conceded that his argument mirrored the one used in the *Brown* case. But he contended that *his* evidence existed, and it proved that children of interracial couples were harmed by the differences in the two races, not from "the inferiority or superiority of either race."

With that, he sat down.

SUMMING UP

The justices then turned their attention to Bernard Cohen. He used the few minutes remaining to him to rebut the state's arguments. First, he attempted to link the two laws in the *Loving* case to the entire Virginia antimiscegenation code. The state legislature, he argued, passed all ten sections as one act, the Racial Integrity Act of 1924. "They are inseparable," he added.

Secondly, Cohen argued that the framers intended the Fourteenth Amendment to be interpreted "in light of changing times and circumstances." If they had intended to exclude antimiscegenation laws from the amendment's guarantees, he said, they could easily have written that into the bill. They did not. Instead, he said, the framers wrote an amendment that was "meant to include equal protection of Negroes. That was at the very heart of it. And that equal protection included the right to marry, as any other human being had the right to marry subject to only the same limitations."

If the Court ruled only on the two sections of the code specifically mentioned in the case, Cohen said, the Lovings—with their marriage voided by the state—would be subject to criminal charges for living together without benefit of marriage. The lawyer argued passionately for "the right of Richard and Mildred Loving to wake up in the morning, or go to sleep at night, knowing that the sheriff will not be knocking on their door or shining a light in their face in the privacy of their bedroom, for 'illicit cohabitation.'" They also had a right, he told the court, "to go to sleep at night, knowing that should they not awake in the morning, their children would have the right to inherit from them, under intestacy. They have the right to be secure in knowing that if they go to sleep and do not wake in the morning, that one of them, a survivor of them, has the right to Social Security benefits."

Concluding his remarks, Cohen once again urged the Court to guarantee those rights to the Lovings and other couples like them by invalidating the state's entire anti-miscegenation code.

U.S. Supreme Court justices gather for a photograph in San Francisco in 1963 during a celebration of Earl Warren's tenth anniversary as chief justice. Front, from left: Justice Hugo Black and Chief Justice Warren. Seated, from left: retired Justice Charles Whittaker, retired Justice Stanley F. Reed, Justices Thomas C. Clark, and William O. Douglas. Standing, from left: Byron White, William J. Brennan Jr., Potter Stewart, and Arthur J. Goldberg (far right). Justice John Marshall Harlan is not pictured. By the time the *Loving* case was heard, Justice Abe Fortas had replaced Justice Goldberg on the Court.

seven
DECISION AND AFTERMATH

on June 12, 1967, Chief Justice Earl Warren delivered the opinion of the Court in the case of *Loving* v. *Virginia*. In a unanimous decision, the justices overturned Virginia's entire code on interracial marriage. "There can be no doubt," Warren read, "that restricting the freedom to marry solely because of racial classifications violates the central meaning of the Equal Protection Clause." The ruling left the Lovings free to live as a married couple in their home state.

The Court rejected both of the state's arguments. It was not enough, Warren noted, for the state to apply equal penalties to black and white partners in an interracial marriage. Because the Virginia code contained racial classifications, the decision stated, the Constitution required a "very heavy burden of justification" for the laws.

In addition, the Court did not accept Virginia's contention that the framers of the Fourteenth Amendment intended to exempt the interracial marriage ban from the amendment's guarantees. Although the debates quoted by the state's attorneys "cast some light" on the discussion, they did not specifically refer to the Fourteenth Amendment and were "inconclusive" at best, according to the decision.

Warren noted that the Court, in *McLaughlin* v. *Florida*, had already ruled that the debates did not support the notion that equal penalties in race-based cases satisfied the equal protection rights requirements of the Constitution. More than just having equal penalties, statutes must not have race classifications that cause "an arbitrary and invidious discrimination." According to the decision, "The clear and central purpose of the Fourteenth Amendment was to eliminate all official state sources of invidious racial discrimination in the States."

Laws that used race to differentiate people could be upheld only when such racial classifications were proved to be "necessary to the accomplishment of some permissible state objective." The objective, warned the ruling, could not be racial discrimination. Warren noted that two members of the Court, Justices William O. Douglas and Potter Stewart, had previously stated (in *McLaughlin*) that they saw no reason for laws to punish people based on the color of their skin.

The fact that Virginia banned only interracial marriages involving white people showed that the laws were enacted "to maintain White Supremacy," according to the opinion. "We have consistently denied the constitutionality of measures which restrict the rights of citizens on account of race."

VIOLATION OF DUE PROCESS

The Court found that Virginia's statutes violated the Lovings' right to due process as well as their right to equal protection, as the appellants had claimed. "The freedom to marry has long been recognized as one of the vital personal rights essential to the orderly pursuit of happiness by free men," Warren wrote. By denying "this fundamental freedom on so unsupportable a basis as [race]"— "so directly subversive of the principle of equality"—the statutes surely deprived "all the State's citizens of liberty without due process of law."

Warren concluded with strong words that left no doubt how the Court stood on the issue of interracial marriage:

> The Fourteenth Amendment requires that the freedom of choice to marry not be restricted by invidious racial discriminations. Under our Constitution, the freedom to marry, or not marry, a person of another race resides with the individual and cannot be infringed by the State.

All nine justices joined in the decision. Justice Stewart also wrote a separate two-sentence concurring opinion. Quoting his concurrence in *McLaughlin*, Stewart wrote:

> I have previously expressed the belief that "it is simply not possible for a state law to be valid under our Constitution which makes the criminality of an act depend upon the race of the actor." Because I adhere to that belief, I concur in the judgment of the Court.

The decision voided laws in all sixteen states that banned interracial marriage.

CELEBRATION AND PROTESTS

Civil rights proponents applauded the decision as a final blow to one of the last of the old South's slavery laws. At a press conference held after the chief justice delivered the opinion, lawyer Bernard Cohen said, "We hope we have put to rest the last vestiges of racial discrimination that were supported by the law in Virginia and all over the country." Historian Philip T. Nash called the decision "a

JUSTICE POTTER STEWART WROTE IN HIS CONCURRING OPINION THAT CRIMES
CANNOT BE BASED ON A PERSON'S RACE.

judicial recognition of the sanctity of marriage and the ability of people irrespective of race to enjoy the protections of the Constitution in their choice of mates."

The decision changed the law of the land, but it did not change Americans' attitudes overnight. When the press reported in September 1967 that the daughter of Secretary of State Dean Rusk planned to marry a black man, Rusk offered to resign if the news threatened to embarrass President Lyndon Johnson. A Georgia native dedicated to the civil rights campaign, Rusk feared that the upcoming nuptials might harm the president's political standing in the South, where opposition to interracial marriage remained strong. Johnson, a major force in the passage of the Civil Rights Act of 1964, gave the offer "no serious consideration," according to news reports. The issue did not die there, however. Some legislators and members of the Board of Regents at the University of Georgia opposed Rusk's appointment to a teaching position at the college in 1969 based on his politics and his daughter's marriage. One legislator was reported to have said that voters blamed Rusk for participating in his daughter's wedding ceremony.

A poll taken in 1968 showed that of thirteen nations, the United States expressed the most opposition to interracial marriages. According to the poll, 72 percent of Americans opposed marriages between whites and blacks.

Although the U.S. Supreme Court ruling clearly made all antimiscegenation laws unconstitutional, the states took their time to rid their books of the offending codes. Virginia repealed the ban in 1968, but did not remove the definition of the races from its statutes until 1975. Florida, Oklahoma, Missouri, Texas, and West Virginia repealed their laws in 1968 and 1969. In several states, the federal government had to seek court orders to force clerks to grant marriage licenses to interracial couples. By

1975, most of the remaining states had eliminated anti-miscegenation codes. A few statutes remained intact for years, even though they could not be enforced. Eleven years after the Supreme Court ruled in the *Loving* case, in 1978, Tennessee citizens finally voted to repeal that state's laws against interracial marriage. Mississippi delayed the removal of its ban on interracial marriages from the state constitution until 1987. And South Carolina retained until 1998 a section in its constitution that barred marriages between whites and anyone with more than one-eighth Negro blood. Alabama became the last state to repeal its law, in 2000, after 60 percent of the voters approved the measure.

The Lovings settled in Central Point, Virginia, in a small white house near the spot where the sheriff raided their bedroom. They raised three children in the house, where Mildred Loving still lives. In 1975, Richard Loving died in an automobile crash not far from the town.

Mildred Loving said she never sought attention and had no interest in being at the center of a landmark Supreme Court case. "It was thrown in my lap," she said. "What choice did I have? We weren't bothering anyone, and if we were hurting somebody's feelings, too bad."

RememBereD TODay

Twenty-five years later, Robert D. McIlwaine, the lawyer who defended Virginia's law before the Supreme Court and lost, dismissed the significance of the decision. "Nobody even remembers it," he said. "It's a footnote to history."

Many people, however, believe the case should receive the attention due a landmark Supreme Court decision. One of them is Ken Tanabe, the son of interracial parents, who has spearheaded a movement to mark June 12 as National Loving Day. First celebrated in 2003, the holiday,

Families Come in
ALL COLORS

Despite the U.S. Supreme Court ruling in *Loving* v. *Virginia*, those who marry across racial lines often face prejudice even in states where marriages between people of different races have never been banned. Stares, disparaging comments, and opposition from friends and family can make life difficult for interracial couples and their children.

As a member of an interracial family, Tamara Moxham learned early on how it felt to bear the brunt of such prejudice. When she was four years old and living in New Hampshire, her mother, a white woman, married a black man. Two years later, they had a baby boy. After the baby's birth, friends in the neighborhood told Tamara they were not allowed to play with her anymore. Their parents had forbidden it because they disapproved of Tamara's new brother. That saddened and confused Tamara, but she soon found other friends whose parents did not share such hurtful views.

An enterprising child, Tamara learned to deal with prejudice in her own way, using humor to illustrate how ridiculous she considered discrimination based on skin color. When Tamara attended college, a friend asked the identity of the handsome young black man in the photograph on her desk. "That's my brother," Tamara replied. The friend, incredulous, insisted that the young man could not possibly be her brother. Tamara remained silent for a moment. Then, with a wave of her hand indicating her white skin, she said, "Oh, you mean this? This is just a birthmark." The friend got the message.

set on the anniversary of the Supreme Court's decision in the *Loving* case, has spread to New York, Chicago, Los Angeles, Seattle, and other cities across the nation. "The primary focus is to fight the racism that still exists today," Tanabe said.

A 1996 TV movie, *Mr. and Mrs. Loving*, highlighted the case, bringing it to the attention of a new generation. Bernard Cohen, one of the two lawyers representing the Lovings in the case, said in an interview after the movie that his clients were not trying "to establish a principle." They pursued the case, he said, because they loved each other. "They couldn't understand how two human beings who were in love with one another and wanted to be married to one another couldn't be married to one another simply because they were of different races," he said.

Today the case is remembered on significant anniversaries of June 12, the day Chief Justice Warren read the opinion in open court. In 1992, on the twenty-fifth anniversary of the decision, the local church awarded Mildred Loving its human rights award. She has received other recognition, including a tribute from the Interracial Family Circle of Washington and the Association for Multi-Ethnic Americans. Both groups formed after the decision to support interracial couples and their families.

Some people still claim the Court made the wrong decision in the case. Sheriff R. Garnett Brooks, who had arrested the Lovings in 1958, told a reporter in 1992 that he thought Virginia's antimiscegenation law "should still be on the books. I don't think a white person should marry a black person. . . . The Lord made sparrows and robins, not to mix with one another."

According to polls, however, most Americans' attitudes toward interracial marriage have changed dramatically since Virginia banished the Lovings from their home. A Gallup Poll taken in 1958 showed that only 4 percent of white Americans approved of interracial marriage. In 2003, a similar poll revealed that 70 percent of whites, 80 percent of blacks, and 77 percent of Hispanics approved of marriages between people of different races. An estimated 450,000 marriages in the United States today—one out of every twenty-five—involve interracial couples. Among them are many prominent people, including Supreme Court Justice Clarence Thomas and his wife, Virginia (who, incidentally, were married in Virginia). According to the 2000 Census, more than three million children of interracial parents live in the United States. Back in 1960, shortly after the Lovings married, the U.S. Census recorded only 51,000 interracial marriages.

Mildred Loving has seen the change. "A few are still very hostile," she said, "but attitudes toward people have really changed. The Old South is going away."

Although the Lovings avoided the limelight and downplayed their role, their daughter, Peggy Loving Fortune, praised her parents for standing up for their right to live together as husband and wife. They made it easier, she said in a 1992 interview with a *New York Times* reporter, for other people to marry, regardless of their race. "To me," she said, "they set the world free to be with whomever they want. I feel it's what they were put on this earth for, that God used them to do what they did."

Banning Same-Sex Marriage

On November 18, 2003, the Massachusetts State Supreme Court, in a one-vote majority, struck down that state's ban on gay marriage and ruled that couples of the same sex had a "fundamental right" to marry. Chief Justice Margaret Marshall wrote in the Massachusetts Supreme Court's decision, "As it did in *Perez* and *Loving*, history must yield to a more fully developed understanding of the invidious quality of the discrimination."

That landmark decision—and the ensuing same-sex marriages in Massachusetts six months later—touched off a heated debate on the legal definition of marriage and who should be allowed to marry. It also has led to comparisons between the Lovings' situation and that of gay couples. Arguments on both sides of the issue echo many of the sentiments expressed four decades earlier in the battle over interracial marriage. In the Massachusetts decision, for example, the court ruled that "the right to marry means little if it does not include the right to marry the person of one's choice, subject to appropriate government restrictions in the interests of public health, safety, and welfare." The state, the court concluded, did not present a "rational reason" for the ban. Lawyers for Massachusetts had argued that recognizing gay unions would undermine marriage and its role in creating a stable society. As in the *Loving* decision, the court noted that scientists did not agree on the issue or on the effects of gay unions on the families involved.

Contrary to the Massachusetts decision, recent court rulings in other states have justified the prohibition against gay marriage with the argument that the ban encourages families to have children and promotes "the well-being" of those children. Dissents issued by opposing judges compare bans against gay marriage to those that barred interracial couples from marrying and say they deprive gay people of their basic rights under the Constitution.

As in the interracial marriage cases, proponents of gay marriage talk of rights and discrimination. "I believe that our Constitution should treat all of its citizens the same, and in this case the court was willing to treat my family differently than other families," said Brenda Bauer, one of thirty-eight people to sue the state of Washington for its Defense of Marriage Act banning gay marriage. The

Washington State Supreme Court overruled two lower courts in 2006 and upheld the ban.

OPPONENTS CALL ON RELIGION

Opponents of same-sex marriage often use religious references when espousing their views—reminiscent of the arguments put forth by opponents of interracial marriage. "Legalizing homosexual 'marriage' will advance the decline of America's remaining morality," James T. Draper Jr. wrote in the *Baptist Press*. "America is mocking biblical morality and turning its back on God."

Responding to the Massachusetts court decision in 2004, President George W. Bush called marriage "a sacred institution between a man and a woman" and said the ruling "violates this important principle." He vowed to work with Congress "to defend the sanctity of marriage."

Not everyone who supports the right of interracial couples to marry believes that the same rights should apply to gay couples. They make a distinction between sexuality and race as a defining factor and argue that gay marriage, like polygamy and incestuous unions, should be banned by the state. "Knocking down bans on interracial marriage did not redefine marriage," said Glenn Stanton of Focus on the Family, a conservative Christian group. "It affirmed marriage by saying that any man has a right to marry any woman under the law. But what same-sex 'marriage' proponents seek to do is to radically redefine the very definition of marriage [and] to say it's not about gender."

Likewise, William Shields, a black Georgia pastor who once participated in civil rights protests, said the Bible permitted interracial marriages but not those between gays. "To connect this to civil rights, to the rights of an individual, is absolutely intolerable," he said. "Being black is not a sin."

WOrLDWIDe Bans

Internationally, several countries have extended some marriage rights to gay couples, but most continue to bar people of the same sex from marrying. In 2001, the Netherlands became the first nation to recognize same-sex marriage. Belgium, Spain, and Canada have since passed legislation allowing people of the same sex to marry and granting them the same marriage benefits as heterosexuals. In December 2005, the Constitutional Court of South Africa acknowledged the marriage of two women. The following November, South Africa's Parliament adopted laws that recognized the right of all same-sex couples to marry in that country. Also in November 2006, Israel's high court ruled that the nation would recognize same-sex marriages conducted elsewhere, though the country does not allow such marriages to take place on its soil.

The European Parliament, in 2000, called for its member nations to grant same-sex couples "rights equal to those enjoyed by traditional couples and families." While not endorsing gay marriage, a number of countries, including Denmark, Greenland, Iceland, Norway, Sweden, Brazil, Israel, Australia, the United Kingdom, and Namibia, grant some rights to same-sex couples. Evangelical Protestant churches, in Africa and elsewhere, and the Catholic Church continue to lead opposition to gay marriage worldwide.

ONLY In MassaCHuseTTs

As of January 2007, only five states in the United States—Massachusetts, New York, New Jersey, New Mexico, and Rhode Island—did not have laws or constitutional amendments that barred marriage between people of the same sex. However, only Massachusetts allowed such marriages to take place; officials in the other five states refused to issue licenses for gay marriages.

Six states—Vermont, California, Hawaii, Maine, Connecticut, and New Jersey—allow gay couples to establish formal relationships and grant them some or all of the benefits allotted to married couples. Of the six, only Vermont, Connecticut, and New Jersey officially recognize civil unions and provide full benefits to gay couples. Bowing to a mandate from the New Jersey Supreme Court, New Jersey legislators sanctioned the unions in December 2006. Under its new law, New Jersey recognizes civil unions performed elsewhere in addition to those conducted in the state. Eight other states, some under court order, offer benefits to partners of gay employees (but do not officially recognize civil unions). Eleven states bar civil unions (and their benefits) as well as banning gay marriage.

Since the Massachusetts court ruling, voters and legislators—incensed over what they view as unwarranted court interference in moral issues overseen by the states—have begun to strengthen bans on gay marriage.

Federal Actions

Congress passed the Defense of Marriage Act (DOMA) in 1996, barring the federal government from recognizing gay marriage. The act, which defined marriage as a union between a man and a woman, also gave states the right to ban gay marriage and not to recognize such unions performed in other states.

Congressional leaders have tried, so far without success, to enact a Federal Marriage Amendment that would add a gay marriage ban to the U.S. Constitution. To be ratified, an amendment has to be approved by a two-thirds vote in both the Senate and the U.S. House of Representatives and by majorities in thirty-eight (two-thirds of) state legislatures.

STATE CONSTITUTIONAL AMENDMENTS

Almost half the states have constitutional amendments banning gay marriage, although the courts have overturned a few of them. After the Massachusetts ruling, eleven states voted to add a gay marriage ban to their constitutions. In November 2004, voters approved amendments to state constitutions that limit marriage to a man and a woman in Arkansas, Georgia, Kentucky, Michigan, Mississippi, Montana, North Dakota, Oklahoma, Ohio, Utah, and Oregon. Missouri and Louisiana adopted similar measures in August and September 2004. A Louisiana state court threw out the ban in that state, however, because the constitutional amendment also prohibited state recognition of civil unions. Louisiana law requires a constitutional amendment to address only one subject. In addition, several states, including Massachusetts, had amendments on the ballot in November 2006 to include a gay marriage ban in their state constitutions.

Nebraska and Nevada already had gay marriage bans in their state constitutions before the Massachusetts court ruling.

State courts in Alaska allowed gay marriages in that state, but voters later approved a constitutional amendment to ban same-sex unions. Likewise in Hawaii, state courts ruled in favor of same-sex marriage, but citizens there passed an amendment that put the matter in the hands of the state legislature, which defined marriage as a union between a man and a woman only.

During elections in 2006, voters in Arizona rejected a ban on same-sex marriage in that state. The close vote marked the first time ever that a gay-marriage ban had been defeated at the ballot box. Voters in seven other states—Colorado, Idaho, South Carolina, South Dakota, Tennessee, Virginia, and Wisconsin—approved constitutional amendments barring marriage between people of the same sex. Colorado also turned down a proposal to recognize "domestic partnerships" (civil unions) between gay partners.

In January 2007 Massachusetts legislators gave the go-ahead to a constitutional amendment that would define marriage as the union between a man and a woman. The amendment needs the approval of at least fifty legislators to win a spot on the state ballot in November 2008. If approved by voters, the amendment would prevent further same-sex marriages in the state. It would not invalidate those marriages that took place between gays after the state court decision made such unions legal.

state statutes
In 1973 Maryland became the first state to pass a law that defined marriage as a union between a man and a woman. Since then, forty-one other states have added such laws to their books, either incorporating the definition or banning gay marriage. Most modeled their laws on the federal Defense of Marriage Act. While Connecticut does not have a specific law banning gay marriage, the state defines marriage as being between a man and a woman in its laws on adoption.

court challenges
State supreme courts in New York and Washington ruled in mid–2006 that states had a "legitimate" and "compelling" interest in banning gay marriage because of society's need to promote families with children. The Washington decision, approved by a narrow 5 to 4 majority, declared that the state "was entitled to believe that limiting marriage to opposite-sex couples furthers procreation, essential to the survival of the human race and furthers the well-being of children by encouraging families where children are reared in homes headed by

children's biological parents." In a stinging dissent, however, Justice Bobbe J. Bridge made frequent references to the *Loving* decision to make the point that the Defense of Marriage Act was discriminatory and violated gay couples' "fundamental basic human rights." Bridge noted:

> In rejecting the plaintiffs' . . . claim, the [Court] rel[ies] on the equal application theory, asserting that because the DOMA restricts men and women equally as classes (because it prohibits both lesbians and gay men from marrying same-sex partners), there is no sex discrimination here. But this equal application theory, as applied to the institution of marriage, has already been rejected by the United States Supreme Court in *Loving*.

In October 2006, California's appeals court took a different view, upholding that state's ban on same-sex marriage. "Courts simply do not have the authority to create new rights, especially when doing so involves changing the definition of so fundamental an institution as marriage," wrote Justice William McGuiness in his majority decision. That ruling is expected to be appealed to the California Supreme Court.

In Maryland, the state's highest court heard arguments on the issue in December 2006. A decision in that case was pending when this book went to press.

Most observers agree that—as in the *Loving* case on interracial marriage—the U.S. Supreme Court will ultimately decide whether or not gay marriage is a fundamental right guaranteed by the U.S. Constitution.

notes

Chapter 1

p. 7, par. 1–3, David Margolick, "A Mixed Marriage's 25th Anniversary of Legality," *New York Times*, June 12, 1992, B-20.

p. 8, par. 1–3, Phyl Newbeck, *Virginia Hasn't Always Been for Lovers: Interracial Marriage Bans and the Case of Richard and Mildred Loving*. Carbondale: Southern Illinois University Press, 2004, 10.

p. 10, par. 1, *Loving v. Virginia*, 388 U.S. 1 (1967).

p. 10, par. 2, *Des Moines Register*, March 31, 1996. Cited in Newbeck, 15.

p. 10, par. 3, Margolick, "A Mixed Marriage's 25th Anniversary of Legality."

p. 13, par. 1–2, Newbeck, *Virginia Hasn't Always Been for Lovers*, 135.

Chapter 2

p. 15, par. 1, Barbara C. Cruz and Michael J. Berson, "The American Melting Pot? Miscegenation Laws in the United States," *OAH Magazine of History*, 15, no. 4 (Summer 2001).

p. 15, par. 2, Cruz and Berson, "The American Melting Pot."

p. 15, par. 2, Michael Lind, "Far From Heaven," *The Nation*, June 16, 2003.

p. 16, par. 1, "Thomas Jefferson and Sally Hemings: A Brief Account," The Thomas Jefferson Foundation, http://www.monticello.org/plantation/hemings contro/hemings-jefferson_contro.html

p. 17, par. 4, Cruz and Berson, "The American Melting Pot."

p. 18, par. 2, Ed Crews, "How Much Is That in Today's Money?" *The Journal of the Colonial Williamsburg Foundation* (Summer 2002). http://www.history.org/foundation/ journal/Summer02/money2.cfm

p. 18, par. 3–4, Cruz and Berson, "The American Melting Pot."

Sidebar

p. 19, J. M. Bloch, *Miscegenation, Melaleukation and Mr. Lincoln's Dog*, 37–42, Schaum Publ. Co., N.Y. 1958; S. Kaplan, "Miscegenation Issue in the Election of 1864," *Journal of Negro History* (34th), 277, July 1949. Cited in *Loving* v. *Virginia*, 388 U.S. 1, appellants' brief, 2.

p. 20, par. 1–2, Appellee's brief, *Loving* v. *Virginia*, 388 U.S. 1 (1967).

Sidebar

pp. 21–24, Constitutional Rights Foundation, "The Fourteenth Amendment," *Bill of Rights in Action*, 7, no. 4 (Spring 1991). http://www.crf-usa.org/bria/bria7-4.htm

U.S. Const. amend. XIV, "The Fourteenth Amendment," The Library of Congress, http://memory.loc.gov/ammem/today/jul28.html

Gitlow v. *New York*, 268 U.S. 652 (1925). Oyez, U.S. Supreme Court Multimedia site. http://www.oyez.org/oyez/resource/case/ 140

Permoli v. *Municipality No. 1 of City of New Orleans*, 44

U.S. 589 (1845).
Slaughterhouse Cases, 83 U.S. 36 (1872).

p. 25, par. 2, *Slaughterhouse Cases*, 83 U.S. 36 (1872).
p. 25, par. 4–p.26, par. 1, *State* v. *Gibson*, 36 Ind. 389 [10 Am.Rep. 42] (1871).
p. 26, par. 3–p. 27, par. 1, *Kinney* v. *Commonwealth*, 71 Va. 284 (30 Gratt.) (1878).
p. 27, par. 2, *Reynolds* v. *United States*, 98 U.S. 145 (1878).
p. 27, par. 3, *Pace* v. *Alabama*, 106 U.S. 583 (1883).
p. 28, par. 1, Cruz and Berson, "The American Melting Pot."

Sidebar
p. 29, par. 2, Kennedy, *Interracial Intimacies*, 24–25, cited in "The Constitutionality of Interracial Marriage" by Williams.
p. 29, par. 3, Cruz and Berson, "The American Melting Pot."

p. 30, par. 1, Randall Kennedy, *Interracial Intimacies: Sex, Marriage, Identity, and Adoption*, New York: Pantheon Books, 2003, 224. Cited in "The Constitutionality of Interracial Marriage: Loving in Thought" by Liza Williams, *Dartmouth College Undergraduate Journal of Law* 2, no. 1 (Winter 2004).

Chapter 3
p. 33, par. 3, Kennedy, Randall. *Interracial Intimacies: Sex, Marriage, Identity, and Adoption*, New York: Pantheon Books, 2003, 24–25. Cited in "The Constitutionality of Interracial Marriage: Loving in Thought," by Liza Williams, *Dartmouth College Undergraduate Journal of Law* 2, no. 1 (Winter 2004).
p. 34, par. 2, "The Murder of Emmett Till," *American*

Experience, WGBH Educational Foundation, PBS, 2003.

p. 34, par. 4–p. 35, par. 1, *Amicus* brief, NAACP, *Loving* v. *Virginia*, 388 U.S. 1 (1967), 2.

p. 35, par. 1, Kennedy, *Interracial Intimacies*, 24–25, cited in "The Constitutionality of Interracial Marriage" by Williams.

p. 35, par. 2, Universal Declaration of Human Rights, United Nations, December 10, 1948, cited in "The Constitutionality of Interracial Marriage" by Williams.

p. 36, par. 1, *Wood* v. *Commonwealth*,159 Va. 963 (166 S.E. 477; 85 A.L.R. 121) (1932).

p. 36, par. 2–p. 37, par. 3, *Perez* v. *Sharp*, 32 Cal. 2d 711; 198 P.2d 17 (1948).

p. 37, par. 5–p. 38, par. 2, Phyl Newbeck, *Virginia Hasn't Always Been for Lovers: Interracial Marriage Bans and the Case of Richard and Mildred Loving*. Carbondale: Southern Illinois University Press, 2004, 98–99.

p. 38, par. 3, *Han Say Naim* v. *Ruby Elaine Naim*, 197 Va. 80; 87 S.E. 2d 749 (1955).

p. 39, par. 1, Newbeck, *Virginia Hasn't Always Been for Lovers*, 98–99.

p. 41, par. 1–4, *McLaughlin* v. *Florida*, 379 U.S. 184 (1964).

Chapter 4

p. 44, par. 1, Appellants' Jurisdictional Statement, *Loving* v. *Virginia*, 388 U.S. 1 (1967), 9–10.

p. 44, par. 2, Phyl Newbeck, *Virginia Hasn't Always Been for Lovers: Interracial Marriage Bans and the Case of Richard and Mildred Loving*. Carbondale: Southern Illinois University Press, 2004, 139.

p. 45, par. 1, Appellants' Jurisdictional Statement, *Loving* v. *Virginia*, 8–10, and Newbeck, 141–142.

p. 46, par. 1, Newbeck, *Virginia Hasn't Always Been for Lovers*, pp. 135–144.

p. 46, par. 2, "A Mixed Marriage's 25th Anniversary of Legality," *New York Times*, June 12, 1992, B-20.

p. 46, par. 3, Newbeck, *Virginia Hasn't Always Been for Lovers*, pp. 135–144.

p. 47, par. 1, Margolick, "A Mixed Marriage's 25th Anniversary of Legality."

Sidebar

pp. 48–50, The Supreme Court Historical Society, http://www.supremecourthistory.org
Administrative Office of the U.S. Courts, http://www.uscourts.gov
Iowa Court Information System, http://www.judicial.state.ia.us/students/6
There is also a diagram on the last Web site.

p. 52, par. 4–p. 53, par. 7, Appellants' Jurisdictional Statement, *Loving* v. *Virginia*, 1.

Sidebar

p. 54, par. 1, Section 20-54, Racial Integrity Statute, State of Virginia.

p. 54, par. 2, Section 1-14, Virginia Code Ann.

p. 55. par. 3–p. 56, par. 1, Appellee's Jurisdictional Statement, *Loving* v. *Virginia*.

Chapter 5

p. 58, par. 1–p. 64, par. 2, Appellants' Brief, *Loving* v. *Virginia*, 388 U.S. 1 (1967).

Sidebar

p. 63, UNESCO, *Statement on the Nature of Race*, cited in *amicus curiae* brief, Japanese American Citizens League, *Loving* v. *Virginia*, 29.

p. 64, par. 4–p. 67, par. 1, Appellee's Brief, *Loving* v. *Virginia*.

p. 67, par. 3–p. 69, par. 1, *Amicus curiae* brief, Japanese American Citizens League, *Loving* v. *Virginia*.

p. 69, par. 2–3, *Amicus curiae* brief, National Association for the Advancement of Colored People, *Loving* v. *Virginia*.

p. 69, par. 4; p. 71, par. 1, *Amicus curiae* brief, Legal Defense and Educational Fund of the National Association for the Advancement of Colored People, *Loving* v. *Virginia*.

p. 71, par. 2–p. 72, par. 1, *Amicus curiae* brief, Catholic bishops et al., *Loving* v. *Virginia*.

Chapter 6
Sidebar

p. 74, Stephen Wyman (former intern in the U.S. Supreme Court Curator's office), interview with the author, September 9, 2006; Public Information Office, U.S. Supreme Court, interview with the author February 8, 2007.

p. 75, par. 2, Clerk of the Court, Supreme Court of the United States, "Guide for Counsel in Cases to Be Argued Before the Supreme Court of the United States, Washington, D.C. (October Term 2003) http://www.supremecourtus.gov

p. 75, par. 4, Phyl Newbeck, *Virginia Hasn't Always Been for Lovers: Interracial Marriage Bans and the Case of Richard and Mildred Loving*. Carbondale: Southern Illinois University Press, 2004, 173.

p. 76, par. 2, Jason McLure, "A Liberal Lion in Winter," *Legal Times*, January 17, 2006.

p. 76, par. 2–p. 78, par.3; p. 80, par. 1–p. 83, par. 3, oral arguments, Philip Hirschkop, *Loving* v. *Virginia*, 388 U.S. 1 (1967).

p. 83, par. 4–p. 86, par. 2, oral arguments, Bernard Cohen, *Loving* v. *Virginia*.

p. 86, par. 4–p. 88, par. 6; p. 90, par. 1, oral arguments, William M. Marutani, *Loving* v. *Virginia*.

p. 90, par. 2–p. 91, par. 5; p. 93, par. 1–p. 98, par. 6; p. 100, par. 1–102, par. 1, oral arguments, R. D. McIlwaine III, *Loving* v. *Virginia*.

p. 96, par. 3, Newbeck, *Virginia Hasn't Always Been for Lovers*, 180.

p. 102, par. 3–p. 103, par. 2, oral arguments, Bernard Cohen, *Loving* v. *Virginia*.

Chapter 7

p. 105, par. 1–p. 107, par. 3, decision, *Loving* v. *Virginia*, 388 U.S. 1 (1967).

p. 107, par. 5, concurrence, Justice Potter Stewart, *Loving* v. *Virginia*.

p. 107, par. 7, Peter Wallenstein, "Race, Marriage, and the Law of Freedom: Alabama and Virginia, 1860's–1960's," *Chicago-Kent Law Review*, 70, 435, cited in Phyl Newbeck, *Virginia Hasn't Always Been for Lovers: Interracial Marriage Bans and the Case of Richard and Mildred Loving*. Carbondale: Southern Illinois University Press, 2004, 189.

p. 107, par. 7; p. 109, par. 1, David Margolick, "A Mixed Marriage's 25th Anniversary of Legality," *New York Times*, June 12, 1992, B-20.

p. 109, par. 2, Marjorie Hunter, "Rusk Was Ready to Quit Cabinet," *New York Times*, September 22, 1967, 35.

p. 109, par. 2, "Controversy Mounts in Georgia Over a Teaching Post for Rusk," *New York Times*, December 23, 1969, 16.

p. 109, par. 3, "U.S. Found Most Opposed to Interracial Marriage," *New York Times*, November 10, 1968, 123.

p. 110, par. 1, Newbeck, *Virginia Hasn't Always Been for*

Lovers, pp. 193–213.

p. 110, par. 3–4, Margolick, "A Mixed Marriage's 25th Anniversary of Legality."

p. 110, par. 5; p. 112, par. 1, Neely Tucker, "Loving Day marks end of interracial ban; Court ruling struck down miscegenation laws," *Grand Rapids Press*, June 18, 2006, A-4.

Sidebar

p. 111, Tamara Moxham, interview with the author, September 29, 2006.

p. 112, par. 2, Anita Gates, "How Love Came to Change the Law," *New York Times*, March 31, 1996, section 12, 3.

p. 112, par. 4, Margolick, "A Mixed Marriage's 25th Anniversary of Legality."

p. 112, par. 5–p. 113, par. 1, Breea Willingham, "Love Is Colorblind in 50 Years," *Times Union*, May 22, 2004, D-1.

p. 113, par. 1, James A. Henretta, *America: A Concise History*, 2nd ed., Boston: Bedford/St. Martin's, 2002, 947, cited in "The Constitutionality of Interracial Marriage: Loving in Thought," by Liza Williams, *Dartmouth College Undergraduate Journal of Law*, 2: no. 1 (Winter 2004).

p. 113, par. 2–3, Margolick. "A Mixed Marriage's 25th Anniversary of Legality."

p. 113, par. 4; p. 114, par. 1, *Hillary Goodridge et al.* v. *Department of Public Health et al.*, SJC-08860, Massachusetts Supreme Court (March 4, 2003–November 18, 2003).

p. 114, par. 3, Associated Press, "Washington court upholds gay marriage ban," July 26, 2006.

p. 115, par. 2, James T. Draper Jr., "First-Person: Whose definition of marriage: God's or man's?" *Baptist Press*,

October 3, 2003.

p. 115, par. 3, "Massachusetts court rules ban on gay marriage unconstitutional," CNN.com Web site, February 4, 2004 http://www.cnn.com/2003/LAW/11/18/same sex.marriage.ruling

p. 115, par. 4–5, Michael Foust, "Bans on interracial marriage, same-sex 'marriage'—parallels?" *Baptist Press,* April 2, 2004.

p. 116, par. 1, Human Rights Watch, *World Report,* 2005. http://hrw.org/wr2k5

p. 116, par. 2, Human Rights Watch, *World Report,* 2001. http://www.hrw.org/wr2k1

p. 116, par. 3, Kavan Peterson, "Washington, New York say no to gay marriage." Stateline.org Web site, March 29, 2005; updated August 3, 2006. http://www.stateline.org

p. 117, par. 1, Laura Mansnerus, "Legislators Vote For Gay Unions In New Jersey," *New York Times,* December 15, 2006, 1.

p. 117, par. 5–p. 118, par. 1, Kavan Peterson, "50-state rundown on gay marriage laws." Stateline.org Web site, November 30, 2004. http://www.stateline.org

p. 118, par. 1, Kavan Peterson, "State legislative activity 2006." Stateline.org Web site, updated August 3, 2006. http://www.stateline.org

p. 118, par. 4, Kavan Peterson, "Seven more states ban gay marriage, but Ariz. bucks trend." Stateline.org Web site, March 29, 2005; updated January 11, 2006. http://www.stateline.org

p. 119, par. 3, Lornet Turnbull and Jonathan Martin, "State Supreme Court upholds gay marriage ban," *Seattle Times,* July 26, 2006, A-1.

p. 119, par. 3–p. 120, par. 2, Bobbe J. Bridge, dissent, *Andersen et al.* v. *King County et al.,* No. 75934-1, Washington State Supreme Court, July 26, 2006.

p. 120, par. 3, Jesse McKinley, "California Court Upholds State's Ban on Same-Sex Marriage," *New York Times*, October 6, 2006, A-16.

All Internet sites accessible as of October 11, 2006.

Further Information

Books

Almonte, Paul, and Theresa Desmond. *Interracial Marriage*. Facts About. Parsippany, NJ: Crestwood House, 1992.

Alonso, Karen. Loving *v.* Virginia: *Interracial Marriage*. Landmark Supreme Court Cases. Berkeley Heights, NJ: Enslow Publishers (July 2000).

Cornelius, Kay. *The Supreme Court*. Your Government: How It Works. Broomall, PA: Chelsea House Pub., 2000.

Grapes, Bryan J., ed. *Interracial Relationships*. At Issue Series. Chicago: Greenhaven Press, 2000.

Heath, David, and Charlotte Wilcox. *The Supreme Court of the United States*. American Civics. Mankato, MN: Bridgestone Books, 1999.

Landau, Elaine. *Interracial Dating and Marriage*. New York: Julian Messner, 1993.

Newbeck, Phyl. *Virginia Hasn't Always Been for Lovers: Interracial Marriage Bans and the Case of Richard and Mildred Loving*. Carbondale: Southern Illinois University Press, 2004.

Patrick, John J. *The Supreme Court of the United States: A Student Companion*, 2nd ed. Oxford Student Companions to American Government. New York: Oxford University Press Children's Books, 2002.

Root, Maria P. *Love's Revolution: Interracial Marriage*. Philadelphia: Temple University Press, 2001.

Sanders, Mark C. *Supreme Court*. American Government Today Series. Austin, TX: Raintree/Steck-Vaughn Publishers, 2001.

Wallenstein, Peter. *Tell the Court I Love My Wife: Race, Marriage, and Law—An American History*. New York: Palgrave Macmillan, 2004.

Audio/Video/DVD

Chen Drammeh, Jessica, director/producer/writer. *Anomaly*, Nyabinghi Productions, in production 2006.

Fox, Jennifer, director/producer. *American Love Stories*, PBS, 1999 (TV series).

____. *An American Love Story*, Zohe Film Productions, 1999 (movie).

Friedenberg, Richard, director. *Mr. and Mrs. Loving*, Hallmark Home Entertainment, 1996 (TV movie).

Irons, Peter, and Stephanie Guitton. "May it please the court: 23 live recordings of landmark cases as argued before the Supreme Court." Sound recording. New York: The New Press, 1993.

Nelson, Stanley, director/producer. "The Murder of Emmett Till," *American Experience*, WGBH Educational Foundation, PBS, 2003.

Web Sites

American Civil Liberties Union.
http://www.aclu.org

Association of Multi-Ethnic Americans, an organization that educates and advocates on behalf of multiethnic individuals and families and works to eradicate all forms of discrimination.
http://www.ameasite.org

FindLaw, U.S. Supreme Court cases.
http://www.findlaw.com/casecode/supreme.html

Interracial Family Circle, providing opportunities for the education, support, and socialization of multiracial individuals and families, transracial adoptive families, and people involved in interracial relationships in the Washington, D.C., metropolitan area.
http://www.interracialfamilycircle.org

iPride, a nonprofit organization interested in the well-being and development of multiracial or multiethnic children and adults.
http://www.ipride.org

Landmark Cases of the U.S. Supreme Court.
http://www.landmarkcases.org

Legal Information Institute, Cornell Law School.
http://www.law.cornell.edu

Mavin Foundation, the mission of which is to celebrate and empower mixed-heritage people and families.
http://www.mavinfoundation.org

Mixed Media Watch, an organization that tracks representations of mixed-race people in the media. The site includes movie reviews, a calendar of events, and a blog.
http://www.racialicious.com

Multiethnic Education Program, provides educators and families with resources and strategies to benefit mixed-heritage children.
http://www.multiethniceducation.org

National Mixed Race Student Coalition, links campus organizations from across the country and organizes the annual National Conference on the Mixed Race Experience.
http://www.mixedstudents.org

Oregon Council on Multiracial Affairs, hosts annual Loving Day celebrations in the Portland area.
http://www.ocma-multiracial.org

Oyez Project: U.S. Supreme Court Multimedia Web site.
http://www.oyez.org/oyez/frontpage

Project RACE (Reclassify All Children Equally), advocates for multiracial children and adults through education, community awareness, and legislation.
http://www.projectrace.com

Supreme Court Historical Society.
http://www.supremecourthistory.org

Supreme Court of the United States.
http://www.supremecourtus.gov

All Web sites accessible as of October 11, 2006.

BIBLIOGraPHY

Articles

Associated Press. "Washington court upholds gay marriage ban," July 26, 2006.

Clerk of the Court, Supreme Court of the United States. "Guide for Counsel in Cases to Be Argued Before the Supreme Court of the United States." Washington, DC (October Term 2003). http://www.supreme courtus.gov

Constitutional Rights Foundation. "The Fourteenth Amendment." *Bill of Rights in Action*, 7, no. 4 (Spring 1991). http://www.crf-usa.org/bria/bria7_4.htm

"Controversy Mounts in Georgia Over a Teaching Post for Rusk." *New York Times*, December 23, 1969, 16.

Cruz, Barbara C., and Michael J. Berson. "The American Melting Pot? Miscegenation Laws in the United States." *OAH Magazine of History*, 15, no. 4 (Summer 2001).

Douglass, Ramona. "The Loving conference June 13, 1992." *AMEA Networking News*, 4, no. 5 (Fall 1992).

Draper, James T. Jr. "First-person: Whose definition of marriage: God's or man's?" *Baptist Press*, October 3, 2003.

Duke, Lynne. "Intermarriage Broken up by Death." *Washington Post*, June 12, 1992, A3.

"The Fourteenth Amendment." The Library of Congress, http://memory.loc.gov/ammem/today/jul28.html

Foust, Michael. "Bans on interracial marriage, same-sex 'marriage'—parallels?" *Baptist Press*, April 2, 2004.

Fulford, Robert. "Mixing races, distilling hypocrisy." *National Post*, December 20, 2003, A22.

Furlong, William Barry. "Interracial Marriage Is a Sometime Thing." *New York Times Magazine*, June 9, 1968, 45, 137–144.

Gates, Anita. "How Love Came to Change the Law." *New York Times*, March 31, 1996, section 12, p. 3.

"Gitlow v. *New York."* Oyez, U.S. Supreme Court Multimedia site, http://www.oyez.org/oyez/resource/case/140

Hartill, Lane. "A brief history of interracial marriage." *Christian Science Monitor*, July 25, 2001, p. 15.

Hunter, Marjorie. "Rusk Was Ready to Quit Cabinet." *New York Times*, September 22, 1967, p. 35.

Kennedy, Randall. *"Loving* v. *Virginia* at Thirty." Speakout.com, February 6, 1997, http://speakout.com/activism/opinions/3208-1.html

King, Colbert I. "Marriage in the March of Time." *Washington Post*, February 12, 2005, A19.

Kristof, Nicholas. "Blacks, Whites and Love." *New York Times*, April 24, 2005, section 4, p. 13.

Lind, Michael. "Far From Heaven." *The Nation*, June 16, 2003.

Margolick, David. "A Mixed Marriage's 25th Anniversary of Legality." *New York Times*, June 12, 1992.

"Massachusetts court rules ban on gay marriage unconstitutional." CNN.com Web site, February 4, 2004, http://www.cnn.com/2003/LAW/11/18/samesex.marriage.ruling

McLure, Jason. "A Liberal Lion in Winter." *Legal Times*, January 17, 2006.

Peterson, Kavan. "50-state rundown on gay marriage laws." Stateline.org Web site, November 30, 2004, http://www.stateline.org

———. "State legislative activity 2006." Stateline.org Web site, updated August 3, 2006, http://www.stateline. org

———. "Washington, New York say no to gay marriage." Stateline.org Web site, March 29, 2005; updated August 3, 2006, http://www.stateline.org

Strasser, Mark. "Toleration, Approval, and the Right to Marry: On Constitutional Limitations and Preferential Treatment." *Loyola of Los Angeles Law Review*, 35:65, 65–100.

"Thomas Jefferson and Sally Hemings: A Brief Account." The Thomas Jefferson Foundation, http://www. monticello.org/plantation/hemingscontro/hemings-jefferson_contro.html

Tucker, Neely. "Loving Day marks end of interracial ban; Court ruling struck down miscegenation laws." *Grand Rapids Press*, June 18, 2006, A-4.

Turnbull, Lornet, and Jonathan Martin. "State Supreme Court upholds gay marriage ban." *Seattle Times*, July 26, 2006.

"U.S. Found Most Opposed to Interracial Marriage." *New York Times*, November 10, 1968, 123.

Williams, Liza. *Dartmouth College Undergraduate Journal of Law*, 2, no. 1 (Winter 2004).

Willingham, Breea. "Love Is Colorblind in 50 Years." *Times Union*, May 22, 2004, D-1.

Audio/Video/DVD

Friedenberg, Richard, director. *Mr. and Mrs. Loving*. Hallmark Home Entertainment, 1996 (TV movie).

Nelson, Stanley, director/producer. "The Murder of Emmett Till." *American Experience*, WGBH Educational Foundation, PBS, 2003.

Books and Reports

Johnson, Kevin R. *Mixed Race America and the Law: A Reader.* Critical America Series. New York: New York University Press, 2003.

Kennedy, Randall. *Interracial Intimacies: Sex, Marriage, Identity, and Adoption.* New York: Pantheon Books, 2003.

Newbeck, Phyl. *Virginia Hasn't Always Been for Lovers: Interracial Marriage Bans and the Case of Richard and Mildred Loving.* Carbondale, IL: Southern Illinois University Press, 2004.

"Supreme Court of the United States" (booklet). Washington, DC: Public Information Office, Supreme Court of the United States, 1979.

Court Cases, Documents, and Statutes

Andersen, et al. v. *King County, et al.* No. 75934-1, Washington State Supreme Court (July 26, 2006). Dissent, Justice Bobbe J. Bridge.

Gitlow v. *New York*, 268 U.S. 652 (1925).

Han Say Naim v. *Ruby Elaine Naim*, 197 Va. 80; 87 S.E. 2d 749 (1955).

Hillary Goodridge et al. v. *Department of Public Health et al.* SJC-08860. Massachusetts Supreme Court (March 4, 2003–November 18, 2003).

Kinney v. *Commonwealth*, 71 Va. 284 (30 Gratt.).

Loving v. *Virginia*, 388 U.S. 1 (1967).

McLaughlin v. *Florida*, 379 U.S. 184 (1964).

Pace v. *Alabama*, 106 U.S. 583 (1883).

Permoli v. *Municipality No. 1 of City of New Orleans*, 44 U.S. 589 (1845).

Perez v. *Sharp*, 32 Cal. 2d 711; 198 P.2d 17 (1948).

Reynolds v. *United States*, 98 U.S. 145 (1878).

Slaughterhouse Cases, 83 U.S. 36 (1872).

State v. *Gibson* (1871), 36 Ind. 389 [10 Am.Rep. 42].

Universal Declaration of Human Rights, United Nations,
    New York, December 10, 1948.
Wood v. *Commonwealth*,159 Va. 963 (166 S.E. 477; 85
    A.L.R. 121).

Web Sites
Administrative Office of the U.S. Courts.
    http://www.uscourts.gov
Association for Multi-Ethnic Americans.
    http://www.ameasite.org
FindLaw (U.S. Supreme Court Cases).
    http://www.findlaw.com/casecode/supreme.html
Landmark Cases of the U.S. Supreme Court.
    http://www.landmarkcases.org
Interracial Family Circle.
    http://www.interracialfamilycircle.org
Iowa Court Information System.
    http://www.judicial.state.ia.us/students/6
Legal Information Institute, Cornell Law School.
    http://www.law.cornell.edu
Loving Day site.
    http://www.lovingday.org
Oyez Project, U.S. Supreme Court Multimedia site.
    http://www.oyez.org
Supreme Court Historical Society.
    http://www.supremecourthistory.org
Supreme Court of the United States.
    http://www.supremecourtus.gov
U.S. Department of State's Bureau of International
    Information Programs.
    http://usinfo.state.gov/products/pubs/rightsof/
    equal.htm

All Web sites accessible as of October 11, 2006.

Index

Page numbers in **boldface** are illustrations, tables, and charts.

African American, 7, 20, 30,
    53, 61, 63–64, 66, 69, **70**,
    78, 80–81, 83, 94–95, 98,
    102
  early American history, **14**,
    15–17, **16**, 19–20, 29, 78
American Civil Liberties
    Union (ACLU), 13, 40,
    42, 44, 47, 52, 57, 75
amicus curiae, 52, 55, 67–72
antimiscegenation, 7, **14**,
    18–20. *See* Interracial
    marriage.

Bazile, Leon M., 10, 43–44,
    46, **47**, 64, 81
Black, Hugo L., 38, 76, 84, 88,
    89, 95, 98, **104**
brief, 51–52, 56, 57–72
Brown v. *Board of Education*,
    13, 31–33, **32**, 38, 47, 53,
    61, 69, 78, 80, 90, 94,
    101–102

certiorari, petition for, 49, 51
Chinese heritage, 28, 30, 78,
    79

civil rights, 10, **11**, **12**, 22, 25,
    31, 33–35, 107, 109, 115
Civil Rights Act of 1866,
    19–20, 61, 66, 81, **82**, 85,
    93
Civil Rights Act of 1964, 12,
    34, 109
civil rights act of 1875, 25
civil rights bill of 1960, 34
civil unions, 114, 117, 119
Cohen, Bernard S., 43–47,
    52, 57, 75, 83–86, 102–
    103, 107, 112
"colored person", 7–9, 76,
    98, 100

Defense of Marriage Act
    (DOMA), 114, 117,
    119–120
Douglas, William O., 38, 41,
    76, **104**, 106
due process clause, 21–23, 25,
    36
Loving case, 44, 53, 59, 64,
    69, 75, 83–84, 87,
    106–107

equal protection clause,
21–22, 27, 31, 36–37,
40–41
Loving case, 44, 53, 59, 62–
63, 69, 75, 77, 84, 87, 91,
95–96, 102, 105–106
same-sex marriage and, 120
eugenics, 28, 78

Freedmen's Bureau Bill,
19–20, 66, 81, 85, 93

gay discrimination, 113, 114
Giaccio v. *Pennsylvania*, 87
Gitlow v. *New York*, 23
Green v. *State*, 26
Harlan, John Marshall, 76,
91, **92**
Hirschkop, Philip J., 44–47,
45, 52, 57, 75–77, 80–84

interracial marriage, **14**, 33,
66, **89**, 97, 111–114, 120
adverse effects of, 100–102
children of, 17–18, 28–29,
36–37, 57–59, **58**, 62, 69,
71, 77–78, 80, 100,
102–103, 111, 113
easing restrictions, 35, 36,
80
states' laws against, 7–9, 15,
17–20, 25, 29–30, 34–37,
39, 40–42, 44, 46–47,
52–55, 58–69, **70**, 71–72,
76–78, 80–88, 91, 93–
96, 98–103, **99**, 105–
107, 109–112
interracial sex, 36, 40–41,

44, 61, 83, 93, 100, 103

Japanese heritage, 28, 30,
67–68, 78, 86, 88, **89**

King, Martin Luther Jr., 10,
11, 33, 34
Kinney v. *Commonwealth*, 26,
66, 78

Lincoln, Abraham, **14**, 15, 19
Loving, Mildred, **6**, 7–10,
12–13, 34, **39**, **42**, 43–46,
53, 55, **58**, 62, 84, 87,
102, 105–106, 110–113
Loving, Richard, **6**, 7–10, 34,
39, **42**, 44–46, 53, 55,
58, 62, 84–85, 87, 102,
105–106, 110
Loving v. *Virginia*, 35, 38, 56,
70
aftermath, 109–110
amicus curiae briefs, 67–72
briefs, 56, 57–67
decision, **6**, **99**, 105–107,
109, 111–114, 120
first steps, 43–47, 51–53,
55–56, 59
oral argument, 75–91,
93–98, 100–102

marriage, legally defined,
114–120
benefits, 53, 77, 103, 116–117
state regulation of, 25–27,
29, 38, 41, 46–47, 65–67,
70, 72, 77, 84–85, 87, 91,
93, 95, 101, 115, 117–120

marry, right to
  interracial, 36–37, 44, 62,
    64, 68, 83, 101–102,
    105–107, 109, 113, 115
  same-sex, 113, 114–120
Marutani, William, 86–88
Maynard v. Hill, 66–67
McIlwaine, Robert D. III, 55,
    64–65, 90–91, 93–98,
    100–102, 110
McLaughlin v. Florida, 40–42,
    47, 53, 83, 87, 93–94,
    106–107
Meyer v. Nebraska, 83
mixed race, 14, 15, 17–19, 47
  children, 17–18, 28–29,
    36–37, 57–59, **58,** 62, 69,
    71–72, 77–78, 80, 100,
    102–103, 111, 113

Naim v. Naim, 38–39, 47, 52,
    55, 65–66, 81
National Association for the
  Advancement of Colored
  People (NAACP), 69, **70,**
    71
Native Americans, 7, 15, 28,
    30, 54, 60, 80, 91
*New York Times v. United
  States,* 50

one-drop measure, 29, 54,
    78, 86, 91

Pace v. Alabama, 27, 40, 68,
    94
Perez v. Sharp, 36–38, 113
Permoli v. Municipality No. 1 of

City of New Orleans, 21
Pocahontas, 15, 30, 60

race, defining, 29–30, 54, 78,
    86–87, 100
racial classification, 105–107
racial composition certificate,
    84–85, 90
racial discrimination, 19–20,
    28, 31, 33, 41, 59–60, 64,
    66, 83–85, 87–88, 94–
    95, 101, 106–107
racial integrity, 17, 26, 28–30,
    36, 46, **47,** 54, 59–60,
    62, 68–69, 71, 77–78,
    80–81, 84, 86–87, 98,
    100
racism, 29, 46, 58, 97, 112
Reynolds v. United States, 27,
    67

same-sex marriage, 113–120
school desegregation, 13, 24,
    31–33, **32,** 38, 61–62, 69,
    90, 94, 101
segregation, 8, 10, 61–62, 64,
    69, 71, 76, 101
sexual classification, 115, 120
Sherrer v. Sherrer, 67
Skinner v. Oklahoma, 83
Slaughterhouse cases, 22, 25
slavery, 14, 15–20, **16,** 29, 42,
    58–60, 76–77, 83, 98, 107
societal attitudes, 96–97,
    109, 112–113
states' rights, 20–27, 90. *See
    also* Interracial marriage.
  regulating marriage, 25–27,

29, 38, 41, 46–47, 54–55,
58–60, 64–67, **70**, 72, 77,
83–85, 87–88, 91, 95,
101, 115–117
State v. *Gibson*, 25
Stewart, Potter, 41, 76, 83, 88,
104, 106, 107, **108**

Trumbull, Lyman, 20, 66, **82**

United Nations, Universal
Declaration of Human
Rights, 35
United Nations Educational,
Scientific and Cultural
Organization (UNESCO)
statement on race, 63,
69, 97–98
U. S. Constitution, 117
Bill of Rights, 23
First Amendment, 23, 24, 36
Fourteenth Amendment,
20–25, 27, 31, 33, 38,
40–41, 46, 59, 61, 65–67,
69, 72, 77, 81, 83 86, 91,
93–95, 98, 100, 102,
105–107
U. S. court system, 48–50
U. S. Supreme Court
antimiscegenation and,
35–39
procedure, 50–52, 73–75

Virginia, 26
An Act for Suppressing
Outlying Slaves, 17–18
race defined, 29, 54, 78, 109
Racial Integrity Act of 1924,

8–10, 29–30, 58–60,
76–77, 80, 90–91, 98,
102, 105
Voting Rights Act of 1965, 34,
90

Warren, Earl, 24, 31, 33, 38,
76, 80, 86, 88, 90–91,
96–98, 100–101, **104**,
105–107, 112
White, Byron, 40–41, 74, 76,
104
white race, 28–29, 54, 62, 68,
78, 80, 86–87, 100
white supremacy, 28, 34, 80,
88, 98, 106
Wood v. *Commonwealth*, 36

about the author

susan DUDLEY GOLD has worked as a reporter for a daily newspaper, managing editor of two statewide business magazines, and freelance writer for several regional publications. She has written more than three dozen books for middle-school and high-school students on a variety of topics, including American history, health issues, law, and space.

Gold's *The Panama Canal Transfer: Controversy at the Crossroads* won first place in the nonfiction juvenile book category in the National Federation of Press Women's communications contest. Her book, *Sickle Cell Disease*, was named Best Book (science) by the Society of School Librarians International, as well as earning placement on *Appraisal*'s top ten "Best Books" list. The American Association for the Advancement of Science honored another of her books, *Asthma*, as one of its "Best Books for Children." She has written several titles in the Supreme Court Milestones series for Marshall Cavendish.

In 2001 Gold received a Jefferson Award for community service in recognition of her work with a support group for people with chronic pain, which she founded in 1993. She and her husband, John Gold, own and operate a Web design and publishing business in Maine. They have one son, Samuel.